CREATE
FUTURE-READY
CLASSROOMS,
NOW!

MEG ORMISTON

Solution Tree | Press

a division of

Solution Tree

555 North Morton Street
Bloomington, IN 47404
800.733.6786 (toll free) / 812.336.7700
FAX: 812.336.7790

email: info@solution-tree.com
solution-tree.com

Visit **go.solution-tree.com/technology** to access direct links to the resources mentioned in this book.

Printed in the United States of America

19 18 17 16 15   1 2 3 4 5

Library of Congress Cataloging-in-Publication Data

Names: Ormiston, Meghan J.

Title: Create future-ready classrooms, now! / Meg Ormiston.

Description: Bloomington, IN : Solution Tree Press, 2016. | Includes

   bibliographical references and index.

Identifiers: LCCN 2015035668 | ISBN 9781936763603 (perfect bound)

Subjects: LCSH: Educational technology. | Education--Effect of technological

   innovations on. | Effective teaching.

Classification: LCC LB1028.3 .O76 2016 | DDC 371.33--dc23 LC record available at
http://lccn.loc.gov/2015035668

_____

Solution Tree
Jeffrey C. Jones, CEO
Edmund M. Ackerman, President

Solution Tree Press
President: Douglas M. Rife
Senior Acquisitions Editor: Amy Rubenstein
Editorial Director: Lesley Bolton
Senior Production Editor: Christine Hood
Copy Editor: Miranda Addonizio
Proofreader: Elisabeth Abrams
Text and Cover Designer: Rian Anderson

This book is dedicated to my number-one cheerleader, my mother, Marta Hart. Mom, you are my rock. Close to home or away at school, my sons, Danny and Patrick, help me catch up and keep up with all things technology. To my husband, Brian—every reference to cloud computing is dedicated to you and all your cloud confusion!

ACKNOWLEDGMENTS

I am a teacher and a presenter but not a natural writer, so trust me when I say you would not be holding this book without the ever-positive Solution Tree team. Douglas Rife, I thank you for your unwavering support during this entire process. I can teach you how to create presentations and use social media, but you taught me how to persevere to make this book a reality. Claudia Wheatley, I will use your words to say thank you for helping me paint on a bigger canvas! In your wonderful Southern way, Claudia, you constantly challenged my thinking and encouraged me along my journey. Sue Kraszewski, you have a true gift in being able to sift through my writing and help me structure the path and direction. You have taught me how to organize and structure my writing. Sue, I thank you. To everyone else on the Solution Tree team, I very much appreciate your hard work to make this book a reality.

Solution Tree Press would like to thank the following reviewers:

Stacey Cool
Chemistry Teacher and
Technology Coach
Golden Valley High School
Merced, California

Jennifer Foor
Teacher and Curriculum Coordinator
Pace Brantley School
Longwood, Florida

DeAnne Hainlen
Coordinator of Instructional
Technology
Eagle Mountain-Saginaw Independent
School District
Saginaw, Texas

Burt Lo
Coordinator of Instructional
Technology Integration
Galt Joint Union Elementary
School District
Galt, California

Susan Prabulos
Technology Teacher
Meadow Lane Elementary School
Lincoln, Nebraska

M. Janet Robles
Spanish Instructor;
Curriculum and Technology
Administrator for L.E.E. Program
Creekside High School
St. Johns, Florida

Jason Rushing
Computer Science Teacher
Humann Elementary School
Lincoln, Nebraska

Visit **go.solution-tree.com/technology** to access
direct links to the resources mentioned in this book.

TABLE OF
CONTENTS

CHAPTER 3
Using Technology Tools for Formative Evaluation

CHAPTER 4
Teaching Metacognition With Technology

CHAPTER 5
Recognizing and Reinforcing the Efforts of
Students, Schools, and Districts

ABOUT THE AUTHOR

Meg Ormiston is an author and a presenter who specializes in transforming teaching and learning through the power of digital tools. She focuses her research on how curriculum can be delivered through the use of visual images, simulations, and multimedia coupled with real-time assessment aligned with the Common Core State Standards.

For more than twenty-five years, Meg has worked with educators to implement changes that improve instructional practices in the classroom. She has an extensive curriculum background, including designing and improving K–12 curricula using digital tools. Meg's specialty is helping educators see that teaching and learning can be done in fresh new ways using technology. An internationally known keynote speaker, Meg engages audiences with powerful digital stories and captivating examples about how teaching and learning can be transformed.

Meg was in the classroom for twelve years teaching grades 2–6 and has also served as a K–8 mathematics, technology, and curriculum coach; a school board member; a professional development specialist; and a grant facilitation specialist. She has authored several books, written numerous articles and blog posts, and collaborated on professional videos. She also is involved in many professional learning communities.

Improving student learning is her central goal for every professional development session. Her classroom background and her wide range of experience give her credibility with teachers, and the practical examples she offers and her upbeat style enrich her presentations and writing to make them especially effective.

Meg holds a master's degree in curriculum and instruction from National Louis University.

To book Meg Ormiston for professional development, contact pd@solution-tree.com.

INTRODUCTION

PEDAGOGY SHOULD LEAD TECHNOLOGY USE IN THE CLASSROOM

In September 2014, I toured a high-performing suburban high school. The rules I saw posted in a classroom included the following: *no phones allowed, no computers open*, and *no touching the SMART Board*. The students, seated in traditional rows, frantically tried to write down everything projected on the slides as the teacher stood at the front of the room reading the text aloud. This approach was not an anomaly used by just one department. After walking the halls and peering into several classrooms, I discovered that this sit-and-get model was the rule rather than the exception. I began to wonder if the digital slideshow-guided lecture would ever die.

The new superintendent took me on this tour to show me what her teachers collectively considered good teaching and learning. In her short tenure in the district, the superintendent repeatedly heard teachers say, "Why should we change? Our test scores are good."

This visit struck me to my core and made me really think about the connections among good teaching and learning (the pedagogy), technology, and systemic change. I wrote this book with the teachers I observed and all others who use the stand-and -deliver method in mind. These teachers teach the way they were taught instead of the way students learn today.

The superintendent has a lot of work ahead of her to help teachers who measure student success by test scores instead of engagement shift their thinking. In order to make such shifts, educators need to start by connecting pedagogy, technology, and change. School systems have long compartmentalized these concepts with different departments working in their own silos of isolation. In the old model, the technology department managed the technology, the curriculum office owned the pedagogy, and the administrators knew about and implemented change. Those traditional roles have become blended. With technology, pedagogy, and change connected, the possibilities are limitless.

The leaders of this movement are the students. They are at the forefront of technology use in education. Teachers need to use their support and guidance to empower all students, regardless of their age, to solve challenging, real-world problems. These trusted teachers are more important than ever, but the large changes necessitated by emerging technology scare many educators and administrators. They must be willing to work together to design and implement a new model so they can provide vital support to their students. When they correctly connect pedagogy, technology, and change, everyone in the school becomes a new teacher, exploring ways to teach and learn in this technology-rich world.

These forces of change, pedagogy, and technology are coming together. Closing the classroom door and repeating the lesson plans of the past is no longer a viable option. Learning becomes transparent, and the world becomes the classroom. There are no limits on learning in this exciting new world! Educators must adopt new teaching methods or pedagogies to transform learning and prepare students to meet the challenges of a changing world and society in which authentic global collaboration and the capacity for continuous learning and relearning are requirements for success. Technology is the connection tool. Pedagogy is how to create change.

Michael Fullan's (2013) book *Stratosphere: Integrating Technology, Pedagogy, and Change Knowledge* is the first place I read about integrating the three forces. I devoured every word of *Stratosphere*, highlighting like crazy and taking copious notes. I loved the message, I understood the purpose, and I agreed with almost every point. Fullan has long been known for his work on change in schools, but this was the first time I had read his work about educational technology. He brought a fresh perspective to the ongoing conversations in the educational technology community by directly connecting teaching and learning, technology, and systemic change. His work helped me clarify my own thinking about the connections and better articulate the relationship between technological tools and learning how to learn. On this connection, Fullan (2013) writes:

> The solution lies in the concentration of the three forces of pedagogy, technology, and change knowledge. If you want to head off destruction, we need to make it all about the learning (the pedagogy part), let technology permeate (the technology part), and engage the whole system (the change part). (p. 74)

With Fullan's work as my foundation, I wrote *Create Future-Ready Classrooms, Now!* as the next step for individuals and school districts who want to connect new pedagogies with current technology to produce the immediate changes they need to prepare students for lifelong learning in a global society. In this book, educators learn about new methods or pedagogies for teaching and learning. It provides the missing link between educational technology theories and effective classroom instruction strategies for the day-to-day use of this technology to enhance learning. Most important, this book teaches educators about learning how to learn in a technology-rich world.

Exploring Technology Use in Classrooms

There is a magical feeling in a classroom when technology is used correctly to engage and empower students and teachers and help them become partners in learning. There is excitement when students have the tools, knowledge, and inspiration to solve real problems that impact others beyond their classroom. Fullan (2013) writes about the importance of this atmosphere of learning:

> Creativity, passion, and purpose must also flourish. We can do all this by gradually building a pedagogy where as they get older, students are more and more steeped in real-life problem solving, guided by teachers as change agents or mentors. (p. 75)

This palpable excitement and energy require the magic of a great teacher. To be great, teachers need all the support they can get from within the system and from experts across the globe. Today, one's personal learning network (PLN) includes not only friends and colleagues but also valuable connections through numerous social networking sites, like LinkedIn, Twitter, Pinterest, and Facebook, among others.

BYOT, One-to-One, and Technology Potpourri

One school district's bring-your-own-technology (BYOT) model makes headlines in the local newspaper, while the private school across town pilots a one-device-for-each-student program, often referred to as *one-to-one*. Some districts have placed laptops in the hands of students for years, while others still struggle with old desktop computers in lab settings. Nearly all districts are in some stage of technology adoption and are exploring different devices, apps, and computer models. Often left out of the conversations around technology are important pedagogical considerations and the change movement.

With this technology potpourri in schools, no single solution will be perfect for all computing needs. Each school within a large district might have a different equipment configuration, making device management a real challenge. Fortunately, devices constantly get smaller and cheaper, making it possible for districts to acquire more of them. The ways devices connect to the Internet are also changing. More districts are working to make buildings wireless, creating even more opportunities for learning unrestricted by location or time.

Besides device issues, districts also struggle with the matter of blocking and filtering content for students and teachers. Schools and districts are all over the board on this issue. In some, filtering is minimal, while in others, it is extreme. Before 2010, the trend was to block nearly every website so nothing bad could happen on the Internet at school. In most parts of the country, districts or schools still block some websites but leave open more web resources and teach students how to use them responsibly. Social media, in particular, challenges districts when it comes to blocking and filtering. The trend follows that of web access in schools as a whole—to allow more social media websites and teach students how to use the apps and websites appropriately.

Technology Models

Just like there is variety in devices and connectivity solutions, there are different technology integration models. Many districts create their own model and use the language to help administrators and teachers talk about levels of technology integration. Regardless of the language used in the model, the goal is to create *common* language with which to discuss lesson design, delivery, and assessment.

The models usually have different levels for lesson development, from very basic and personal to complex, and for publishing and sharing globally. Staff members are often at different levels with their own technology skills, making differentiated and personal professional development very important when technology and pedagogy come together. No matter what language a district adopts, it must strive with its integration model to create a common understanding of what quality projects look like. At the highest level of reflection, teachers should give students more of a voice and choices as they tackle real-world problems and create content for an authentic audience that extends beyond the classroom. Students should direct their own learning path using the technology resources.

The Substitution Augmentation Modification Redefinition (SAMR) model, developed by professor Ruben Puentedura, a respected professor and thought leader in the world of educational technology, is a popular technology integration model adopted by many school districts (Puentedura, 2006). Puentedura's very insightful website and blog *Hippasus* (www.hippasus.com) offers relevant research and examples. The SAMR model provides the framework to create a common language for what effective teaching and learning look like in the classroom. SAMR includes four stages of technology integration—(1) substitution, (2) augmentation, (3) modification, and (4) redefinition—for transforming and enhancing instruction with technology.

Substitution is the lowest level of technology integration, meaning that the technology simply substitutes for the way the lesson was always presented before. For example, if a teacher projects a worksheet on a screen using a document camera, that is substitution; it is still the same lesson and worksheet, just projected.

The next stage is *augmentation*, meaning the teacher improves the lesson using the technology tool. For example, instead of reading aloud a section of the textbook, the teacher creates a multimedia presentation that includes a number of primary-source documents about the topic.

Moving closer to the goal, *modification* of the lesson means the teacher significantly alters the task using technology resources. A good example of this is the use of a Google Form to streamline data collection from students before, during, or after a lesson. The teacher and students use technology, and the form keeps the data nicely organized in a spreadsheet. However, the project is not out the door yet, because the data set is still the same group of students.

Redefinition is the top level and the ultimate goal for designing technology-rich lessons and quality student projects. I use the phrase *get the project out the door*, meaning the lesson is designed to reach an audience beyond the students sitting in the classroom. A good example of this is the use of a student blog, meaning the students publish their work online using a blog platform. To connect with a wider audience, the teacher broadcasts the published work using social media websites, such as Twitter, Facebook, or Pinterest, and invites people to comment on the student work.

The SAMR model (see figure I.1, page 6) has emerged through Puentedura's work with school districts worldwide at all phases of implementation of educational technology programs. I refer to the SAMR model frequently throughout this book.

Publication of Student Work

It is very important for teachers, students, administrators, and parents to understand the importance of getting student-created projects out the door. To connect pedagogy and technology, students must be active learners while building and creating authentic projects with real-world significance, and most important, sharing their work with a global audience. Creating these opportunities for engagement inside and outside the classroom helps teachers prepare students for the future workplace.

The concept of getting projects out the door is foreign to many educators. Illustrating the transformation of traditional lessons to exemplar lessons helps teachers understand what this model would look like in their classrooms. Once teachers and students begin to get feedback from an authentic audience, they will very quickly see the importance of publishing student work.

Teaching in the Cloud

In order to restructure lessons to be technology rich and collaborative, both teachers and students must understand cloud computing. Most teachers already teach in the cloud, though they may not use the term *cloud computing*. According to

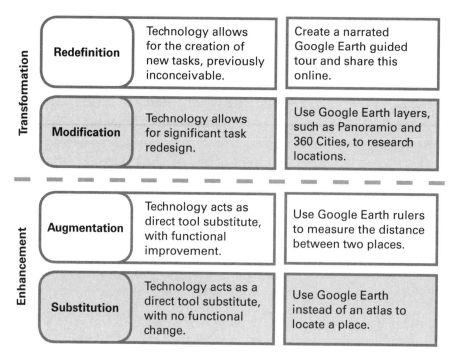

Source: Puentedura, R. (2014). SAMR, learning, and assessment. Accessed at www.hippasus.com /rrpweblog/archives/000139.htm on October 7, 2015.
Figure I.1: SAMR model.

Merriam-Webster's Online Dictionary, cloud computing is a noun defined as "the practice of storing regularly used computer data on multiple servers that can be accessed through the Internet" (Cloud computing, n.d.). Chances are, most have already done this in their teaching practice as well as their personal lives to some extent.

A few examples of cloud computing teachers may already use include:

- Accessing email (for example, https://mail.google.com)

- Storing files in a file-hosting service (for example, www.dropbox.com)

- Working with Google Drive documents (https://drive.google.com)

- Checking social media sites (for example, www.facebook.com)

- Sending tweets on Twitter (https://twitter.com)

- Sharing pictures on an image-sharing site (for example, http://picasa .google.com)

- Connecting with others on professional networking sites (for example, www.linkedin.com)

Accessing and using cloud resources are part of teaching and learning today. Because these services are online, you don't need to install software, making it possible to access documents from any Internet-enabled device 24/7. Before cloud computing, educators could save their documents and files to the school server, which is sometimes called *the network*. The network administrator would typically back up the server nightly to keep documents safe. While they were indeed safe, in most districts, teachers could not access documents outside of school. Emailing the document home was about the only way to work on a document outside of school, and this practice went on for years until USB flash drives became affordable. Now, with cloud storage document solutions, teachers can open and edit almost any document on any device without flash drives or email.

Using the cloud has important implications for teaching and learning. Specifically, the cloud allows everyone to virtually get on the same page and collaborate online without attaching documents through email. For example, groups of students can work on the same Google Doc from any Internet-enabled device. One student, the document owner, creates a document and shares it with other users to whom he or she gives editing rights. When any user saves the document, it saves to Google's servers, often referred to as the cloud.

Working in the cloud happens at all levels of education and in the workplace. We must prepare students to work collaboratively using a variety of cloud-based tools, allowing them to create and connect in exciting new ways.

Google Drive is one cloud tool that I reference throughout this book. I explain particular features as they connect to the relevant pedagogy. I have included Google tools specifically because many districts have already transitioned to or are planning to transition to using Google Apps for Education, but little has been written about how to connect these tools to teaching and learning. Other schools use a cloud-based system like Microsoft Office 365. All the activities presented in the book can be used for any cloud collaboration system.

Collaborating Using Technology

Face-to-face and cloud-based collaboration, active learning, and social networking are all part of modern teaching and learning. Several instructional methods fall under the term *active learning*, including cooperative learning, problem-based learning, and collaborative learning. Active learning is best described as placing the focus and responsibility for learning on the learner. It often contrasts with the traditional lecture method in which students passively collect the information from the teacher. With or without technology, students and teachers must be active learners. The use of technology and the Internet makes it possible for students to become globally active learners who collaborate without geographic and spatial boundaries.

Many educators still do not see the purpose of connecting with social media. Meanwhile, students actively collaborate using a variety of social media platforms, including Twitter, Facebook, Pinterest, Instagram, Vine, and YouTube. Platforms may come and go, but the collaboration online continues. Therefore, today's educators must be willing to embrace social media–based collaboration to enhance their students' active learning.

Social Media for Professional Development

Twitter is my number-one source for personal professional development. In 140 characters or fewer, I connect with other passionate educators across the globe. I have many followers I know from my face-to-face professional development work, but I also have countless others who make up what I call my *research and development team.*

Growing a talented Twitter team or PLN has taken me years, but the results have been well worth the effort. The vast majority of my followers and the people I follow are educators who share my passion for teaching and learning with technology. Because I have so many experts in my Twitter stream, I feel like my own resident researchers are just a tweet away. If I get stuck on a problem, I can rely on my team to connect me to information and examples of best practice.

Document Sharing and Permissions

In this world of social media pedagogy, technology, and change, sharing what we learn benefits everyone. Much of that sharing takes place online through social networking websites and in the cloud. In the past, many teachers kept their best work to themselves, hoarding their lessons and best practices in old filing cabinets. Today, it is vital that educators develop a culture of sharing, opening documents to critical groups by granting permission to others to view their work. It is time to get everyone on the same digital page and collaborate.

Extending the School Day

Getting everyone on the same page using technology tools and websites finally makes it possible to extend the school day. Students and teachers can stay connected in safe and secure learning management systems (LMSs) or open that communication using one of the various backchannel methods that I will introduce in chapter 1. Outside of school, students can continue to create group projects by sharing documents, developing shared presentations, and even making their own movies online.

Reading This Book

Create Future-Ready Classrooms, Now! formalizes the connection between effective instruction and the meaningful use of technology in classrooms. Based on the findings of current research, it integrates the most critical pedagogies with cutting-edge technology, identifying specific instructional strategies and matching them with the most effective technology solutions for immediate classroom implementation.

This book helps teachers understand what these pedagogies look like in the classroom and how to use the digital tools available. Keeping the focus on quality instructional strategies is essential. *Create Future-Ready Classrooms, Now!* is filled with instructional strategies and technology resources explained in language accessible to a wide audience with varying levels of technological knowledge and skill and is adaptable to classrooms with any configuration of technological devices.

I structured this book like my face-to-face professional development sessions, and I organize my professional development sessions like I would run my classroom. In my direct instruction, I strive for engagement every four or five minutes, using a balance of conversation, reflection, summarization, creation, research, exploration, and establishment of global connections. My purpose in writing this book is to share my passion and present the information in such a way that readers can replicate the strategies in their own classrooms and adapt the pedagogy to their curricular needs. I designed this book to be practical and useful to busy teachers everywhere.

You can use this book with collaborative teams in professional learning communities (PLCs) or during short segments of professional development time, like early start days or shared planning time. Groups of teachers are invited to select a section of the book to highlight during a faculty meeting that will be helpful in creating desired schoolwide change. To help spark discussion, at the end of each chapter, reflection questions encourage deeper thinking on the topics. The book's companion website at **go.solution-tree.com/technology** also offers several additional resources.

The chapters in this book are organized in a way that scaffolds the skills, beginning with technology tools teachers can start using immediately. For example, chapter 1 discusses specific tools, apps, and strategies for providing specific and timely feedback. As the book progresses, the reader will gain information about additional technology tools and instructional strategies to use in the classroom. The content is organized in a practical way, making it easy to immediately apply the ideas, concepts, and strategies to your work as an educator.

Chapter 1 details instructional practices for giving useful feedback to students and provides research-based evidence to support the importance of this feedback as well as connecting to the global community. The feedback loop designed to increase student achievement includes websites, technology tools, and devices. Center stage in this chapter is the concept of backchanneling, including multiple technology platforms that allow teachers to start providing effective feedback immediately.

Chapter 2 furthers the concept of providing quality feedback and focuses on helping students create nonlinguistic representations using a variety of technology tools. Students can use media for deeper learning and explain ideas by creating multimedia projects. This chapter details the ethical use of digital resources, including copyright-free images. It also covers locating, creating, and editing podcasts and music as part of the video creation process and explains the digital storytelling process, along with suggestions for how students can create their own digital stories using various websites, apps, and software resources.

Chapter 3 introduces new technology-rich strategies to provide formative evaluation feedback to students. Some of these follow a game-show-type of format, while others allow students to draw pictures and submit them to the teacher through an online interface. This chapter also covers creating and sharing pencasts, or digital, interactive note taking, as another way to provide formative evaluation feedback with technology. Educators also learn how to freshen up the exit slip instructional strategy with new, easy-to-manage technology solutions.

Chapter 4 discusses metacognition, or thinking about one's own thinking. It also reviews the concept of screencasting (that is, the capture of action on a computer screen) and follows with information on creating one's own projects. In addition, it presents a variety of additional tools to help students visualize their thinking, including creating tag clouds, graphic organizers, and infographics.

Chapter 5 offers a whole new twist on recognizing and reinforcing student efforts. I introduce technology innovations, including the major concept of engaging students with the typical elements of game play, also known as *gamification*. Creating and issuing digital badges and encouraging students to collect them is a hot new way to recognize students, and several technology resources are available to bring the idea to the classroom and beyond. This chapter also includes the topics of streamlining the feedback process and using social media to broadcast great news.

Chapter 6 features the concept of collaborative and cooperative learning. Collaboration is a theme throughout this book, but in this chapter, I introduce new technology tools and resources to prepare students for success in higher education and careers. I also cover creating, managing, and providing feedback to cooperative groups using technology. By building global cooperative groups using social media and video conferencing, teachers can extend learning beyond the walls of their classrooms. This chapter also discusses sharing the work of cooperative groups using social media and technology.

The epilogue concludes this book by looking ahead and realizing the possibilities for teaching and learning in a digitally rich world. It reiterates the importance of collaboration in a constantly changing society, as well as the necessity of providing quality feedback regardless of the technology platform. Here, I remind educators that the tools, apps, software, and websites they use are in continual flux, and the only constant is change itself.

Finally, a handy appendix lists all the technology resources from this book. I have organized the resources into categories and listed the websites for each resource, along with a short summary of the app, website, software, or platform. In addition to the appendix, technology tools will be added and updated on the companion website for the book (**go.solution-tree.com/technology**). When my PLN shares a new technology resource with me, I will share it with you online. Let's continue to learn together!

CHAPTER 1

Providing Specific and Timely Feedback

This chapter was in the outline stage in April 2015 when I had the opportunity to have lunch with my college-age son, Patrick, and a group of his friends. Through creative questioning, I collected a lot of information about how the students feel about teacher-to-student feedback, student-to-student feedback, and feedback from others using social media. This lively conversation made it very clear to me that not every classroom provides students with specific and timely feedback.

Patrick's friend Jackson said that in one of his classes, the professor lectures and the class takes notes most of the time. The professor reserves the last five minutes of class for questions; otherwise, the students can schedule a meeting during office hours. Jackson shared that he has trouble getting all the notes down in time and understanding the topic. The professor uses PowerPoint to guide the lecture but does not share the presentations with students. The only feedback Jackson has had from the teacher is grades—weekly quiz grades, grades on homework, and grades on tests. After the last high-stakes test, Jackson's grade was not what he or his tutor expected. All he had was his grade when he met with his teacher to go over the test; and even after the meeting, he still was not clear about what he needed to work on.

Patrick, on the other hand, is taking a class in which the professor spends very little class time on lecture; the students conduct most of their work in small groups. The groups work together in class and ask questions of the professor when needed. They have a rubric and very clear expectations for each project. The groups give a presentation every week, and during the presentations, the other students and the professor use a Google Doc to give specific feedback and ask questions of the group. Patrick added that the feedback has helped him become a much better presenter, and he feels more confident in his public speaking.

Another friend, Carlye, wished that her teachers could be more like her golf coach when it comes to feedback. Her golf coach helps her break down her golf swing and focus on just one thing at a time. And while she practices, Carlye receives specific feedback on that skill from her coach. Carlye pointed out that her coach has completely changed her swing, helping her have a great season.

Ben and Zach, meanwhile, are in a class together. They laughed about the class, which they said that they like, even though they have no idea how they are doing. Every few weeks, they get a score posted to the online grading system; but even as finals approach, they are not sure how to study for the exam.

Patrick mentioned that he gets very timely and specific feedback from followers on social media, who comment on the videos he films and posts to his YouTube channel, but it is a whole different world in the classroom. With thousands of views and likes on his YouTube channel and even more on his shared photos on Instagram, he was excited to take a photography class. On the first night of class, Patrick shared his YouTube channel with his teacher, as well as the recent still and video projects he had created using a new drone. The instructor said he didn't believe in sharing work online and informed Patrick that in his class he would not permit the use of GoPro cameras or drones. He expects students to follow the syllabus and learn how to take pictures that are not autofocused using the new technology. As a social media devotee would say, #WhyChange.

Another friend, Jonah, knows that I love technology, so he was eager to share that he had two instructors that semester who do not allow anyone in the classroom to use any technology during the class. When the instructor set out the class norms, she explained that the no-computer rule was to prevent students from checking Facebook during her lectures. Jonah thought this was funny because Facebook was about the last social media site he would ever check. He also mentioned that this instructor was the only one he had who did not use the college's LMS. She told the class that she liked to grade real papers and did not have the Internet at home.

This conversation reveals two major concepts educators should be aware of if they want to improve student learning: students crave specific, timely feedback; and technology can be a powerful tool to help them learn.

Before exploring technology tools, websites, or other resources, it is essential to understand *why* feedback is so important to students. Making the time for feedback always challenges busy educators, but, as the following section explains, it is one of the most effective strategies to increase student achievement and engagement.

Realizing the Importance of Feedback

Why is feedback important to students? In *How to Give Effective Feedback to Your Students*, Susan Brookhart (2008) writes:

> Feedback says to a student, "Somebody cared enough about my work to read it and think about it!" Most teachers want to be that "somebody." Feedback matches specific descriptions and suggestions with a particular student's work. It is just-in-time, just-for-me information delivered when and where it can do the most good. (p. 1)

Feedback is part of the formative assessment process. Educators should refine their specific feedback skills through ongoing professional reflection, along with other formative assessment skills like setting and communicating clear learning targets and helping students set their own learning goals.

Brookhart (2008) continues:

> The purpose of giving immediate or only slightly delayed feedback is to help students hear it and use it. Feedback needs to come while students are still mindful of the topic, assignment, or performance in question. It needs to come while they still think of the learning goal as a learning goal—that is, something they are still striving for, not something they already did. It *especially* needs to come while they still have some reason to work on the learning target. (pp. 10–11)

This Brookhart quote reminds me of all the times feedback reaches the learner only *after* he or she has completed the assignment and typically doesn't care anymore and has moved on to other things. Feedback needs to reach learners in time for them to use it for improving their performance.

Using Different Forms of Feedback

John Hattie and Helen Timperley (2007) identify four types of feedback teachers can offer students.

1. Feedback about the task
2. Feedback about the processing of the task
3. Feedback about self-regulation
4. Feedback about the self as a person

When providing feedback about a task, teachers should focus on what is correct or incorrect about student work, including its quality. A task rubric allows the teacher to give feedback in very specific language and recognize which students need reteaching on a given topic. Task feedback offers students a chance to expand their ideas and project direction and should correct misconceptions as well as include comments about structure, neatness, and overall design. Because task feedback is specific to an assignment, the feedback may not transfer to other tasks.

Process feedback from the teacher should focus on the strategies students used to tackle the task. He or she should focus on the information gathered, how it's organized, and possible alternate strategies for approaching the task. Through this specific process feedback, the teacher helps students create strategies that they can apply in various subjects and problem-solving situations.

Feedback from the teacher about self-regulation directs students to pace and monitor their own learning progress. Self-directed learners start to develop and internalize a set of personal patterns that they can independently apply to new learning situations. As learners acquire the new internal self-regulation strategies, they may need external suggestions and help from the teacher in the form of feedback.

Teachers must be especially careful when providing feedback to students as individuals, which might include statements about their personal traits and characteristics. This type of feedback does not focus on the task, and it can even hinder students' ability to learn the specific problem-solving skills that other types of feedback develop. When providing feedback, teachers must be specific and identify the growth each particular student has made instead of what I call *fluff feedback*. For example, feedback about goal setting and accomplishments based on these goals is better than providing a general statement unrelated to the task.

Teachers can offer students many types of feedback, but the most powerful feedback in the classroom is from the students to the teacher (Tovani, 2012). This feedback allows the teacher to see the lessons through the eyes of the students. Teachers can then use the information they gather to plan the next steps in the learning progression. Collecting and reflecting on feedback from students is one way for teachers to dramatically improve their instructional practice. However, many teachers, especially new teachers, are afraid to take the risk and ask for it. For example, a teacher might ask students to anonymously share how they would improve a lab activity to gather feedback and inform future instruction. Using an online chat or backchannel, he or she also might reflect on the lesson in real time and, based on the online feedback, make real-time adjustments during the lesson.

In addition to teacher-to-student and student-to-teacher feedback, there also is student-to-student or peer feedback, though the value of this feedback may be questionable at times. In an *Educational Leadership* article, Hattie (2012a) states,

"Most of the feedback that students receive about their classroom work is from other students—and much of that feedback is wrong" (p. 18).

I would agree that inside the classroom, feedback among students might not be accurate if it's about a low-level task in which students are not invested. For example, if students peer-edit a story that they don't really care about, the feedback might be inaccurate. Compare this to the feedback students might give each other during a video game. Outside of school, that real-time feedback is specific, relevant, high quality, and timely because it could mean survival and success.

However, students receive or give feedback regularly outside of the classroom, and this feedback is often more on target. For example, in the world of online video gaming, feedback is usually very specific, accurate, and focused on solving difficult problems with the goal of moving through the levels of the game. Online gaming environments also rely on specific feedback among team members to survive and thrive within the game. The feedback among peers is accurate and direct because success in the game demands it.

Gaming is a real-world activity in which the feedback loop plays an important role. Noted neurologist, teacher, and author Judy Willis (2011) writes that video games are not the enemy of education; instead, they are models for the best teaching strategies. Students need to use what they learn in authentic ways so they can see their progress, and visual progress is an integral part of video games. Feedback is ongoing during most multilevel video games, and players often receive tokens or sound effects when they succeed, priming them for more success. According to Willis (2011):

> When the brain receives that feedback that . . . progress has been made, it reinforces the networks used to succeed. Through a feedback system, that neuronal circuit becomes stronger and more durable. In other words, memory of the mental or physical response used to achieve the dopamine reward is reinforced.

In the classroom, when students work toward challenging but achievable goals, they focus and persevere to tackle them, especially when a feedback system is in place. Willis (2011) adds:

> One way to help each student sustain motivation and effort is to shift progress recognition to students themselves. This can be done by having students use a variety of methods of recording their own progress toward individualized goals. Through brief conferences, goals can be mutually agreed upon, such as number of pages read a week (with comprehension accountability), progression to the next level of the multiplication tables, or achievement of a higher level on a rubric for writing an essay.

In this way, students can harness the motivating power of feedback rewards to continue their learning progression.

Using the Power of Specific and Timely Feedback

The better a teacher communicates expectations and clear, measurable outcomes, the more effective and specific the feedback, both positive and corrective, he or she can offer the learner. At the very beginning of the planning process, the teacher should ask, "What do I want my students to know and do as a result of this lesson?" He or she must clearly define the objective in content-specific language, and the objective must align with the benchmarks, standards, and local curriculum.

The second question a teacher should ask in the planning process is, "How will the learning be measured?" The teacher must explicitly state to students and their parents both the objective and the expectations. He or she can then direct the feedback to meet expectations and achieve objectives.

The third question a teacher should ask is, "How will I provide feedback before, during, and after the student completes the lesson?" Specific feedback during the lesson allows the student to immediately change direction and make corrections instead of waiting until after the assignment is completed. At that point, the feedback is not as important and certainly not as relevant, because the student will not have the opportunity to learn in the moment and make adjustments to the assignment.

Educational expert Grant Wiggins (2012) writes about goal-referenced feedback, "Effective feedback, requires that a person has a goal . . . and receives goal-related information about his or her actions" (p. 13). He also differentiates between information and feedback: "Information becomes feedback if, and only if, I am trying to cause something and the information tells me whether I am on track or need to change course" (p. 13).

Students can receive feedback in a variety of ways, informally and formally, both inside and outside the classroom. As noted by Jan Chappuis (2012), timing is critical: "Effective feedback occurs during the learning, while there is still time to act on it" (p. 36). Feedback is essential during the entire learning process, not just at the end of an assignment. Peter Johnston (2012) writes, "When we give a grade as part of our feedback, students routinely read only as far as the grade" (p. 64). Johnston is right on here—feedback after the assignment is completed is lost when the student returns home, and all he or she reports is the letter grade, minus the feedback.

Some of the feedback between teachers and individual students should be kept private. One way to maintain a secure feedback loop is to record comments in a shared Google Doc. The teacher can create a Google Doc and share it with the student. The document then becomes a safe place for a feedback exchange between teacher and student. Depending on the purpose of the feedback, the teacher may also share this document with support teachers or parents. Using the Google Doc, instead of a pencil-and-paper solution, allows everyone in the feedback loop to access the information in real time from any Internet-enabled device. It streamlines the feedback process because all the data are in one place, and everyone involved can reflect on the information to look for patterns and successes.

Backchanneling to Promote Ongoing Feedback

One way to provide specific, timely, and continual feedback is through backchanneling. *Backchanneling* is a term used for an ongoing conversation. TodaysMeet (https://todaysmeet.com) defines it as follows:

> The backchannel is everything going on in the room that isn't coming from the presenter. The backchannel is where people ask each other questions, pass notes, get distracted, and give you the most immediate feedback you'll ever get.

In a classroom, teachers can use backchanneling throughout a class period. To get started, the teacher connects the projector to his or her computer and shares with students the web address for the backchannel. At their desks, students participate in the online conversation with Internet-enabled devices. If there are not enough devices for each student to have one, the teacher can group students around available devices. If school policy permits, backchanneling also works well on most smartphones.

Tracy, a sixth-grade social science teacher, uses a backchannel every day with her students. She starts each class period with a challenging focus question about the lesson to see what students already know about the topic. Students immediately get started answering the question. Tracy then quickly scans students' responses to check students' background knowledge before beginning the lesson.

As Tracy starts the lesson, she encourages her students to pose questions in the backchannel. She structures her lessons by building in collaboration time about every five minutes. As the small groups discuss the question she has given them, she quickly checks the backchannel to see what questions they have posted. She can individually address students' questions or build the answers into the next segment of instruction.

After a few minutes of collaboration, Tracy asks each group to summarize the conversation in the backchannel as she watches on her computer. The lesson continues with collaborative breaks throughout. Near the end, Tracy asks the students a question that serves as a formative assessment in the form of an exit slip using the backchannel platform.

Tracy then shares with the class that she will check the backchannel between seven and eight o'clock that evening in case students have additional questions or need help with homework. Tracy also encourages students to answer and clarify their classmates' questions. As she prepares lessons for the next day, she can reflect on the types of questions students ask in the backchannel and adjust her planning and pacing, as needed, for each of her classes.

Now that the backchannel is part of her instructional practice, Tracy can't imagine teaching without it. After using the backchannel for a few days, students feel very comfortable working in the online environment. They also report that they go back through the backchannel to help prepare for chapter tests. (T. George, personal communication, May 6, 2015)

By using the backchannel, Tracy gets very specific feedback as she presents the lesson. Students also get their questions answered in real time, often by other students who offer immediate support and guidance.

Benefits of Backchanneling

I have been using a backchannel during my face-to-face professional development sessions since about 2010, and it has become a vital component of my teaching strategy. I use a variety of technology tools beyond the ones I explain here, but whatever I use, I need some type of technology solution that connects me to participants. I often refer to my backchannel as the connective tissue that keeps our group together. Backchannels allow me to provide important information efficiently. For example, I can post a complicated website address as a hyperlink instead of asking teachers to waste time typing. The backchannel also serves as a running record of conversations.

The backchannel also helps me improve my own performance. I use it to reflect on my presentations. After a session, I can look back to see if the participants picked up my key points, allowing me to adjust my content and topic sequence accordingly. It also creates an archive of the class dialogue that I can use as evidence of participant engagement.

Backchanneling isn't for everyone; some people learn best using pencil and paper to record their ideas and thoughts, and some people are distracted by the typing going on all around them. However, it has been my experience that most people engage much better with the message I deliver when the backchannel opportunity is available to them.

Backchannels allow the teacher to reach everyone, not just the hand-wavers in the front row. They enable him or her to provide very specific feedback to the whole group or individual students based on what they share online. One student's question could help someone else in the room. The best backchannels are not completely teacher focused; instead, the students provide feedback to each other and share resources without interrupting the lesson.

Backchannels can even allow students who are absent from class to participate in the conversation. A teacher shared with me that one of her students had to travel to another state for medical treatment, and the backchannel helped him engage during his time out of the classroom. Talk about being a connected teacher! She was able to provide immediate feedback and facilitate the comprehension of a student in need from thousands of miles away, helping him stay involved with the instruction back in school.

Collaborative Backchannels Inside and Outside of School

Teachers can use backchannels in very creative ways. A superintendent shared with me that every Sunday evening, his daughter's fourth-grade teacher has a thirty-minute meeting with students and their families using Twitter as a backchannel. The classroom teacher shares what to expect during the upcoming week, offers great resources, and answers any questions students or parents have. If parents can't attend the live session, they can review the conversation, which is archived on the class hashtag on Twitter.

Privately, the superintendent followed up with the classroom teacher, asking her why she would give up precious time on Sundays. The teacher answered that by engaging with the families like this on Twitter, she has dramatically reduced her email communication. In addition, she has stopped publishing her weekly paper newsletter, opting instead for archiving her weekly tweets on the website Storify (https://storify .com) and sharing the link and page with her students' families.

For this teacher, the backchannel commitment saves time. It allows her to give critical feedback to students and at the same time, document and archive parent and student communication without any additional work.

Another talented primary-grade teacher asserted that she could not teach without multiple backchannels. When I asked her why she needed more than one, she said that she creates a backchannel for each group, and while she works with a small reading group, she can use her iPad to monitor the progress of the other groups. That immediate, quick check provides a way for the other small groups to ask questions without physically interrupting the teacher's reading lesson. Talk about multitasking!

This teacher loves the strategy because she can look at what groups are doing from any computer, meaning she doesn't have to lug a pile of papers home each night. In this case, the teacher set up multiple rooms on TodaysMeet and labeled the groups with her last name and group number (1–10). Regardless of which students are in group 1 that day, they know which room to use for their backchannel. Each group of students has a laptop and a set of questions to answer as they read and discuss their literature circle books. Students collaborate and give each other feedback before they summarize and record their answers in the backchannel.

A high school principal explained to me that his staff uses a backchannel for all their PLC work. Each team creates a Google Doc and shares the document with the team as well as the principal. From any Internet-enabled device, he can open the document, see what the group is working on, and provide feedback in real time instead of waiting for a scheduled meeting that may be weeks later. In the past, he would have to sort through piles of meeting notes and then follow up with feedback days or weeks later. He has vowed never to go back to the old model of paper meeting minutes.

A director of teaching and learning in a large school district talked about how she has conducted all of her Common Core State Standards (CCSS) curriculum realignment through a backchannel she and her colleagues created using Google Docs. Teachers love that they can do the work from any Internet-enabled device, with all their great ideas saved in one shared document. The teachers have reduced their face-to-face meeting time, are not being pulled out of class, and feel more organized than ever before.

The director appreciates that she doesn't have to drive all over the district to attend meetings, and at any moment, she can give timely and specific feedback to each group. Before they adopted this backchannel system, the committee members communicated with each other by attaching documents to email. Now the amount of email is reduced, and everything is organized and accessible to everyone in real time. The director also shared that they used to refresh the curriculum on a two- to three-year cycle, and now they update the curriculum daily. For example, a website used for one lesson might suddenly change or a better resource could be available, and that resource would be added to the shared curriculum document immediately instead of waiting years to make the change.

A high school advanced placement (AP) teacher shared with me that he holds what he calls "office hours" on TodaysMeet the night before a test to answer any last-minute questions. The feedback he provides to one student can help the entire class. This teacher said his students' test scores have improved dramatically since he started using this strategy. The students also like this approach because they can participate from any Internet-enabled device, including their cell phones. This teacher uses TodaysMeet for his office hours, but any backchanneling solution would work for this application. This teacher archives the backchannel in a transcript at the end of the year to use as evidence of student engagement, to include in his professional portfolio, and to restructure lessons for the next year based on student questions.

The staff at a very large high school, meanwhile, uses a shared Google Doc as their backchannel to track parent communication. The entire staff shares the document, and when anyone contacts a parent, the backchannel records the communication. They use the data they collect to look for trends, identify potential concerns, and increase parent involvement.

Group Norms for Backchannels

Before starting a backchannel with students or colleagues, and even before selecting a technology tool to create the experience, it is critical to establish group norms that clearly define expectations for participants. Each participant must understand group communication norms that define how the group should behave in the online environment.

Examples of group norms include the following.

- Use proper spelling and grammar, not text language.

- Use classroom-appropriate language.

- Always post messages using your own name.

- Stay on topic, and follow instructions from the teacher.

- Be respectful to classmates online and offline.

Equally important are the consequences participants will face if they do not follow the norms. It is good to establish these guidelines before getting started so that students know both what they can expect and what is expected of them. Students can access the backchannel inside and outside of school, so make sure they understand the same rules apply whenever they access it.

Backchanneling Platforms

There are many different ways that technology can support the concept of backchanneling. For this book, I have identified three of my favorites. Organized from easiest to use to most complicated, first is the website TodaysMeet (https://todays meet.com); the second is Google Docs; and the third is Twitter (https://twitter.com). Each of these communication platforms is free, open to everyone, and accessible on any device connected to the Internet.

TodaysMeet

TodaysMeet is the top choice for getting started right away at generating feedback and sparking discussions without requiring students to remember a login name or password. Like Twitter, there is a limit of 140 characters per post, helping students and teachers get to the point with a short message. The layout and formatting of the free website are very easy to see on various devices.

On TodaysMeet (https://todaysmeet.com), the teacher is prompted to create a room. He or she selects a name for the room that is not already taken and then decides how long to keep the room open (from one hour to one year). Several features provide the teacher with control over the messaging in the room. It is important to note that data can be deleted without warning, so users need to create a transcript, copy it, and save it if the data are important.

After the teacher creates the room, he or she can copy the web address and share it with students. When they follow the link, the website prompts students to enter their names, and then they are ready to participate in the online conversation. Students can take part in the backchannel conversation even if they are not in class on a particular day. The teacher should prepare key questions about the lesson for students to respond to and keep an eye on the backchannel to address any questions or concerns before, during, and after the lesson.

On the TodaysMeet platform, the feature called *transcript* allows the teacher or students to archive the information shared in the backchannel. Teachers can save the transcript as evidence of student engagement, feedback, and a reflective tool, and also to capture shared resources. Students can copy the transcript to help them study for an upcoming exam.

Google Docs

Teachers can use a Google Doc, a part of Google Drive, to create a backchannel in a controlled online environment. Google Drive is a cloud-based productivity suite that currently provides word processing (to create documents such as letters and reports) and other template-based applications, such as slides, spreadsheets, folders, drawings, and forms. Dictionary and translation programs are also built in. The owner of the document manages access by keeping it private or selecting options to make it open to selected users or even publicly to anyone on the Internet.

The default document ownership setting for everything in Google Drive is private. If the document owner wishes to share it, he or she must change the settings to share the document with particular users. The sharing principles are the same in all Google Drive applications (spreadsheets, slide presentations, and so on).

Many schools use Google Apps for Education, meaning the teacher and student login addresses are also their access to Google Drive and other features. Even in schools that don't use Google, teachers can start using Google tools by visiting https://mail.google.com to create a Gmail account. This free account provides an email address through Gmail, but it also lets teachers access Google features, including Google Drive.

To clarify, each Google Doc can be shared in three ways.

1. Publicly with anyone on the Internet

2. With anyone with the specific link

3. Through specific email addresses that the owner of the document enters

For each shared document, the owner has the option to allow editing, viewing, and commenting, and these options can be different for different invited users. If the teacher shares the document by adding email addresses, the participants receive an email with the link they can click to instantly become part of the document and begin working. If the teacher shares the document publicly on the web or with anyone who has the link, he or she needs to make sure all participants have the link.

A quick way to provide the link is to copy and paste the web address to TodaysMeet. Then invitees can just click and get to work. At the time of this writing, the Google Drive links are difficult to manage because of the complexity of the characters and the length of the address. One way to shorten the link is to use a URL shortening website like TinyURL (http://tinyurl.com). TinyURL and sites like it process complicated web addresses to create shorter, easier-to-manage web URLs that link to the same web locations. By comparing and contrasting, it's plain to see that the shorter address is much easier to type into a web browser if needed. For example, the complicated web address https://docs.google.com/spreadsheet/viewform?usp=drive _web&formkey=dERFbjRpcy1hVV9nenRSVENpNmJiSlE6MA#gid=0 can become http://tinyurl.com/k5u73fk with just a few clicks.

Once they are logged into Google Drive, teachers are ready to create the backchannel using Google Docs. In the lower right corner is a red button with a plus sign. This is the Create button. Users can also click New on the left. Next, they select Document, label the document, and insert a table. Users can create a table with two cells across (two columns) and about twenty down (twenty rows). These cells will help focus the collaborative work of the group. In the left column, the teacher posts a question, and students respond to that specific idea on the right. Teachers add cells to the table as they add more topics to the backchannel. The table layout helps to keep groups focused and organized around different topics.

Teachers can use the table to give structured feedback to the entire class before, during, and after the lesson. They tag each addition to the document with the student's name, making it possible to follow up with individual students as needed. All the comments around the topic are continuously and automatically saved into the

Google Doc, streamlining the feedback process for the teacher. The teacher can comment one time, and the feedback reaches the whole class simultaneously.

Kaizena is an add-on app that allows teachers to leave voice comments in a shared Google Doc, which can be a huge time-saver for teachers interested in giving quality feedback to students. To install the Kaizena app, open Google Drive, click on the Create button, and select Connect More Apps. Search for Kaizena, and select Connect. Once the app is connected through Google Drive, Kaizena installs a menu for easy access to the application through the Add-Ons menu.

Using Kaizena is fairly easy. The student creates a document and shares it with the teacher. The teacher opens his or her Google Drive and locates the student document in the Shared With Me folder. The teacher opens the document and selects Kaizena from the Add-Ons menu. Next, the teacher highlights part of the document to direct the feedback to a specific section of the writing, and the option to record appears as a microphone icon. Other options for leaving feedback include inserting a virtual sticky note or a link to an outside website right in the student's document. The teacher continues to leave feedback in voice comments throughout the student's document. The student opens the document on his or her device at home or school and can listen to specific feedback, which appears color-coded for easier identification. What a great way to add a personal audio touch to the feedback loop! It also can save teachers countless hours of printing and writing out feedback.

When students share work via a Google Doc, it allows the teacher or peers to comment, chat, and annotate student assignments. Before introducing these features to students, however, teachers should review the class norms and consequences for failing to adhere to them.

In the Google Drive environment, a student's or teacher's name is connected to everything he or she posts. It is important for students to understand that nothing is anonymous. Each school district that becomes a Google Apps for Education district can access a management dashboard that the administrator can use to enable and disable features, including student email. For example, some districts use the management system to limit the chat feature.

Anyone who has been invited to the Google Doc can post comments. There are two types of comments in Google Docs: general comments and text-specific comments. General comments, or overarching comments that apply to the document as a whole, are located in the upper right corner next to Share. Teachers can add text-specific comments under the Insert menu. To use this feature, highlight a block of text and insert a comment (or use *control* + *alt* + *m*). The comment appears on the right side of the document and remains connected to that specific part of the text.

When the student logs in, comments appear embedded in the document, providing specific feedback throughout. Students can review a record of the comments by clicking on the Comment button and making the changes. This works similarly to the Track Changes feature in Word. This running record helps the student grow as a writer, while the teacher can see how he or she used specific feedback to refine his or her work. This is a great way to drill into the document and give that critical, specific feedback. The Track Changes feature many people use in Microsoft Word is similar to the one available in Google Docs called Suggesting. An editor also can type text, highlight words or passages in the document, and change formatting. During the revision process, the student reads the comments that teachers and peers have added, and after making the needed changes, he or she clicks on the comments to address them.

Another feedback method is the chat feature. This feature is only available when multiple people are sharing a document and are concurrently online. Contributors make edits in the document while chatting about the changes, providing feedback in real time. Groups collaborating on a document can work together from any part of the globe using any Internet-enabled device in real time. In the classroom, small groups of students can peer-edit and refine documents using the various commenting tools.

Twitter

Backchanneling was a term new to me when I started using Twitter many years ago. I quickly learned how powerful this concept is for providing and gathering specific feedback. Backchanneling as a concept did not catch on right away because many people thought it was rude not to look at the presenter. Now people tweet through presentations, sharing key points and resources with the Twitterverse. Often, people who backchannel share pieces of the session, including key points the speaker makes, ideas, and questions. In these posts, people may include the conference hashtag to help other people outside the room follow along with the session. A hashtag is a code for the conference that someone makes up and shares with the group. This is just one way that hashtags can be used to organize information about groups, activities, and events. Preceding the code is the hashtag (#) sign. Some examples are #edchat, #4thchat, and #scichat. Visit the website http://cybraryman.com/edhashtags.html for a comprehensive list of education hashtags.

Twitter is a very public way to backchannel, so it is important that everyone who chooses this option understands that other people can take a tweet and send it out to their followers. This is called *retweeting*, or *RT*. If Twitter is the feedback method of choice to use with students, teachers must remind them to be careful about what they share online, including personal information and images of others. Each student also needs an email address to create an account, which can be a problem if the school does not assign email addresses.

A few ways to use Twitter with parents and students include sharing deadlines; operating a homework hotline; broadcasting class, school, or current events; connecting with outside experts; and following age-appropriate chats through the use of hashtags.

Twitter is a free service. You can set up an account on Twitter by first choosing a username and login password. Next, you are asked to complete an online profile. Many people read profiles to decide whether to include others in their network. Adding a photo of yourself can help people in the network to remember you. You can find people using the Find People function. It allows you to search by usernames (for example, mine is @megormi) or real names, if you know of others on Twitter with whom you want to connect. Submit a request to follow your selected individuals. Once they accept your follow request, you are connected, and they will see your posts. Finally, grow a network by looking for people who would bring value to conversations of interest. As your network grows, so too will the power of collaborative conversation.

As long as there is an Internet connection, students can backchannel with learning partners across the globe, creating authentic collaboration opportunities. The teacher can structure this feedback into the lesson, making it possible for students to get specific feedback from the teacher as well as other experts and learners around the world.

Providing Feedback in a Learning Management System

A learning management system (LMS) is an online collaborative environment designed to connect teachers, students, and sometimes parents. There are many different platforms in the market, with more emerging based on the demand and feedback.

The systems range from free to very expensive enterprises. Some of the platforms work for K–12 education, but Blackboard, for example, is often used in higher education. Regardless of the platform, it is best practice for all teachers in a building to use the same LMS so students are not confused by differences in platform features from class to class. Instead of looking at the specific features of each platform, this section focuses on the common features teachers can use to provide feedback to students and to streamline classroom management.

Some LMSs adopted by K–12 districts include the following.

- **Edmodo:** www.edmodo.com
- **OtusPlus:** http://otusplus.com
- **Schoology:** www.schoology.com

- **Canvas:** www.canvaslms.com
- **Blackboard:** www.blackboard.com
- **My Big Campus:** www.mybigcampus.com

In most LMS systems, the teacher creates an account and separate classes. When a class is created, a code is generated, which is shared with students. Some LMS systems also allow parents into the class as an observer, limiting their access to the work assigned and completed by their own child. When the student or parent enters the code, he or she is connected to that teacher and the specific class period.

After the teacher posts an assignment, students open the task on their devices, complete the work, and if the assignment is digital, submit it to the teacher within the LMS. Working in an LMS helps teachers and students stay organized, keeping all the work within the environment and out of email.

Discussion boards are part of the LMS environment, making it possible for teachers to provide specific feedback to students. Many LMSs have an environment similar to the interfaces found on Facebook and Twitter. Teachers can send announcements to the group or messages and assignments to specific students, making it easier to differentiate instruction. Some platforms also have additional tools, like highlighters and digital ink, that teachers can use to provide feedback to students.

Using Technology Innovations for Feedback

Video conferencing has long been used in business, but now many teachers connect with experts and collaborate beyond the walls of the classroom. FaceTime, Skype, and Google Hangouts are a few of the popular apps or software for this service. Each one can broadcast experts into the classroom to chat and pose questions, providing very specific feedback to students.

As an example, two middle school teachers in my school were redesigning a science lesson about plants. From their professional development session in the Chicago area, they Skyped with a forester from Oregon to ask about project suggestions and collect very specific feedback, which they used for lesson design. Social media is a great way to tap experts in the local community, including friends and family, and to reach experts across the globe.

In addition to screen sharing, participants can use built-in features to record the on-screen work of a student or an outside expert. Teachers can embed and play a YouTube video for the group to watch and then use the chat option for questions or to clarify key points. The Hangout environment also includes a direct connection to Google Drive, simplifying the process of document sharing without having to leave the environment.

Khan Academy

Sal Khan started the Khan Academy (www.khanacademy.org), a free online education organization, to help his extended family as they struggled with topics in mathematics, science, history, and much more. Khan created what I call *screencast videos* and posted them to YouTube. A *screencast* is the result of when technology is used to capture what is on the screen as a teacher works through a lesson. The software or website used to record the lesson then packages the screencast into a movie that users can play on virtually any device. (Screencasting is covered in depth in chapter 4.)

People outside Khan's family discovered his video collection, and its popularity grew. With some early funding from various sources, the Khan Academy was born. Today, there are more than three thousand lessons, translated into many languages, with multiple funding sources. The Khan Academy is committed to offering a free, world-class education to all. Embedded assessments provide immediate feedback, hints, and suggested follow-up videos based on the results of practice problems.

The feedback loop in the Khan Academy is very interesting. Students—or their parents, if the students are younger than thirteen—can create an account with Khan Academy. They earn badges based on their online work and acquire energy points based on the amount of time they spend in the Khan Academy environment. Students go on to earn additional badges based on how many videos they watch, how many practice problems they complete, and their online activity.

Parents, teachers, and outside coaches can follow student progress. The Khan Academy offers a log of learning progress complete with advanced analytics that include how many minutes students spent on the videos, practice problems attempted, and badges earned. The data are presented in a variety of ways, making it very easy for students and teachers to get a snapshot of their online activity. This engaging feedback facilitates reteaching and enriches classroom activities.

One third-grade teacher explained that his students love using the Khan Academy in the classroom and at home because it makes learning fun. His entire class chased one student who had raced ahead and was doing mathematics at about the eighth-grade level. She was gathering many badges, and the other students were putting in more hours just trying to catch up. When the teacher studied the classroom data, he drilled down to find which individual students were struggling and with what, and then he used this information to differentiate instruction in the classroom.

Digital Data Collection

Technology offers several platforms for collecting data so teachers can readily access and easily use them for timely feedback.

Google Forms

One feature of Google Drive is Google Forms. Students and teachers can create all types of forms to collect data from a variety of sources, such as surveys, data-collection sheets, and quizzes. Several different formats are available, including multiple choice, text, paragraph text, checkboxes, scales, and grids.

There are three parts to a form, and moving from layout to layout can be confusing. Google calls the first part the *live form*; I call it the *pretty part* because the user can add a background. The live form is the view students see when they complete and submit the form. As soon as a student submits the form, Google automatically populates a spreadsheet with the data; this is the second part. The third part of the form is the summary of the data. All the parts are saved into one document in Google Drive. The form opens in the spreadsheet view; to move to other views, users click on the form menu header and select the view they are interested in working with. This form is just a way to streamline data collection, which the teacher studies to provide students with specific feedback.

Polling Solutions to Collect Feedback

The website Poll Everywhere (www.polleverywhere.com) allows users to create and share polls with an audience. On the free plan, forty people can respond to a poll using text messages, Twitter, or a web browser. The simple interface has two formats to create the poll—multiple-choice and free-response answers. After a teacher uses a poll with one class, he or she can clear the results and then use it again for additional students (up to forty). A PowerPoint and Keynote feature make it possible to insert the poll directly into a slide presentation.

After users create an account on Poll Everywhere, the site prompts them to enter a question and select the format for the answer. Teachers should be sure to review the norms of online behavior established earlier with students, especially if they select free-response answers. After a user creates the form, the site saves it in the user's account. When the teacher is ready to use the form with students, he or she should start the form and select the option for full screen. Students then answer the questions using their digital devices.

Poll Everywhere provides quick assessment opportunities before, during, and after lessons to help pace instruction and check that each student understands the content. Teachers can use the data collected to differentiate instruction and reteach as needed. These data also can serve as a basis for further discussion of the topic or for reflection and feedback.

The data collected on Poll Everywhere are not easy to save and manipulate after the session. The most robust classroom polling systems are often called *classroom clickers* or *student response devices*. Classroom clicker systems make it easy for the teacher to collect, save, and organize data. The teacher can immediately observe the overall success of the class. After the lesson, he or she can drill down to the specific data collected for each student. Chapter 3 provides additional details about student response devices.

Technology and Feedback

Time management is always a challenge for busy educators, but by using the various technology resources covered in this chapter, they can streamline the process of data collection and organization.

Douglas Fisher and Nancy Frey (2012) specifically address the topic of making time for feedback and using the data collected wisely to maximize student progress.

> Although responding to students' work is time-consuming, teach-
> ers invest the time because of the effect it can have on student
> learning. But they need to make good use of this time. They can
> do this by focusing on errors rather than mistakes, noticing pat-
> terns in errors, addressing targeted and global errors, and guiding
> learners to increased understanding. (p. 46)

When the data are organized and centralized in a spreadsheet, analysis is so much more efficient. Teachers are able to provide specific, quality feedback to individuals as well as groups of students, saving precious time both inside and outside of school.

Despite all their benefits, technology-based feedback systems should not completely replace traditional feedback methods. Teachers still need to structure time to provide face-to-face feedback to students. Time also should be allotted for students to work in groups and provide feedback to each other. No matter how many devices are in a classroom, face-to-face interaction is still incredibly valuable and critical to higher-level learning.

This chapter discussed a variety of technology tools, platforms, apps, and websites teachers can use to collect and keep track of student information and provide specific and timely feedback. Technology tools will continue to come and go. They will appear on the market as the next best thing, and something else will ultimately replace them. However, the importance of providing effective feedback that students can immediately apply to improve their work is critical to student success. Technology can be used to provide feedback more effectively and efficiently and in a way that engages students in the process.

⚡ Team Discussion Questions

Use the following questions for personal review, professional development, or as a discussion guide for collaborative groups in your PLC.

1. After reading the research about providing feedback to students, how would you summarize the reasons that feedback is so important?

2. Before you read this chapter, what was your background knowledge about Google Drive, and what did you learn from this chapter that you can apply specifically to your work?

3. Within Google Drive, what are three features you would like to learn more about?

4. What was your background knowledge about backchanneling, and how would you describe the concept to someone who has never heard of it?

5. Although there are many ways to backchannel, I specifically detailed three technology platforms in this chapter. Please compare and contrast these three platforms.

6. Craft three to four sentences to summarize your thoughts on seeking feedback from outside experts, including your opinion of the value of this practice.

7. Please list and explain three specific strategies you would like to apply after reading this chapter.

8. I could have included many additional technology solutions in this chapter. If you were to add an app, website, or technology platform, what would you add, and why?

9. What is your plan to disseminate the information you learned from this chapter to colleagues?

10. This chapter specifically focuses on feedback between teachers and students. In your role as a teacher, what exactly would you want to know more about or have clarified?

CHAPTER 2

Creating Nonlinguistic Representations for Deeper Understanding

Nonlinguistic representations include whole-body movement, audio experiences, multimedia productions, models, coding, building, drawing, sculpting, singing, animating, woodworking, cooking, graphic organizers, avatar design, and so on. Each is an effective tool to increase student achievement and integrate technology.

This chapter is about creating nonlinguistic representations with a focus on deeper learning. The critical component of effective multimedia use is to keep the focus on the content, making sure students fully understand the expectations before the lights, camera, and action begin. The tools, apps, and websites will continue to change, but educators can quickly adapt carefully planned projects to make use of the latest and greatest technology.

This chapter also highlights the importance of creative expression in student learning and explains why students should create nonlinguistic representations. It provides strategies for connecting prior knowledge to new experiences and, specifically, building vocabulary using technology resources. It also explains the digital storytelling process and the locations of online resources for immediate use; ethical use of online content; collaborative planning; creating, presenting, and publishing multimedia presentations; and assessing multimedia projects.

The information in this chapter can help teachers gain the necessary skills to support students as they plan, create, and publish their work using a variety of technologies. I encourage teachers to stop as they work through this chapter and try to build, create, and make models to share with students, colleagues, friends, and family.

Our classrooms have traditionally been tightly focused on reading, writing, and lecturing; this chapter offers a fresh, new way for students to express their ideas using different media. To illustrate how you might introduce and integrate this idea, I offer an anecdote from a professional development experience I had at a local middle school in August 2014.

After tabulating a student interest survey, a middle school leadership team learned that many students enjoy creating movies and taking pictures outside of school. The team decided to create learning opportunities using these images and have students create more multimedia presentations of their own.

The team wanted to learn about possible projects and then create examples to show the students, so I conducted a day of professional development for them focused on creating content and developing rubrics for assessment. The cross-curricular team wanted students to create a variety of projects using different technology tools, apps, and websites. They identified five different types of projects to develop: multimedia biographies, videos displaying vocabulary development, photo-essays, digital story-telling, and photojournalism.

Multimedia biographies replaced the long-standing family tree poster project in the language arts classes. The family tree was already well developed as the final poster project, so the team made a few changes to the rubric and then spent time exploring the apps, websites, and applications students could select from to create their final projects. The three language arts teachers selected different applications and created their own multimedia biographies. They used a rubric as the guide and made adjustments as needed.

The science teachers were looking for ways to help students who have trouble understanding the difference between two related topics in a unit. These teachers decided to have the students create a movie to explain how the concepts work in their lives outside of school. They specifically included the use of pertinent vocabulary in their rubric. The teachers set to work creating the videos.

The Spanish teacher wanted to have groups create photo-essays about places they would study throughout the year. Her goal was to use the student-created photo stories to open each unit. She created a list of items to include in the photo-essay, such as a music clip to play along with the images.

A group of teachers wanted to create persuasive digital stories about careers in mathematics and science. These teachers planned to connect with a local business to allow students to interview and shadow scientists and engineers at work. The final student products would become part of the annual career fair. The teachers also planned to archive the projects on a website for students to access any time.

The social science teachers wanted students to create a photojournalism project about real issues in the local community. The teachers decided to have the groups brainstorm issues they felt were important to study and then start researching. Groups earned a higher grade if they found an expert on the topic whom they could include in the video.

The day flew by as each group used images and multimedia to create projects. Near the end of the day, we came back together for show-and-tell and to debrief. All team members agreed that they enjoyed creating the projects, and they all felt that students would welcome the change. The teachers also shared that they learned that providing a clear project overview and assessment rubric would structure the students' content focus and keep it where it should be—on using media to share what they learn as a result of the research. I was surprised when the groups talked about giving students a choice about which technology apps, websites, and applications they would use. After a day of exploring and observing the different tools in action, they were much more comfortable with students selecting how they wanted to create their final projects.

Defining the Importance of Nonlinguistic Representations

In many traditional classrooms, teachers rely heavily on language-mediated tasks; students predominantly demonstrate what they have learned through writing or answering questions verbally. Many students who experience difficulties with linguistic representations struggle academically. Schools emphasize language mediation —simply put, reading, writing, and listening. However, educators are increasingly aware that including more nonlinguistic representations when presenting lessons positively impacts many students, especially those who struggle with linguistic representations. Students also benefit from the freedom to create their understanding of a topic in ways that extend beyond pencil and paper.

Every individual is different in how he or she processes and shares information linguistically and nonlinguistically. Many students thrive in a heavily language-mediated classroom, while other students struggle. Teachers can increase student achievement by balancing lesson delivery between linguistic and nonlinguistic representations. By offering students options in demonstrating what they know and can do as a result of their learning, teachers help more students succeed in the classroom.

Sir Ken Robinson (2009), in his book *The Element: How Finding Your Passion Changes Everything*, addresses the importance of variety in teaching and learning:

> Academic ability is very important, but so are other ways of thinking. People who think visually might love a particular topic or subject, but won't realize it if their teachers only present in one, nonvisual way . . . These approaches to education are also stifling some of the most important capacities that young people now

need to make their way in the increasingly demanding world of the twenty-first century—the powers of creative thinking. (p. 14)

Most student projects use a combination of linguistic and nonlinguistic representations; the key to balance is letting students choose what they want to create. Through the appropriate use of technology, students and teachers can create and share many different types of linguistic and nonlinguistic representations, including screencasts, movies, animations, simulations, stop-motion video, movement, digital image manipulation, and more.

With technology tools in the hands of students and teachers, the possibilities for creating nonlinguistic representations in the teaching and learning process expand dramatically. Students and teachers can share these new creations, along with traditional lessons, beyond the walls of the classroom, using the innovative technology covered in this chapter. The idea of creating and publishing is new to many teachers. I often describe this as *messy learning*. In a digitally rich classroom, everyone's final product is unique. I believe that, as educators, we should guide and support students as they build and create, but we must also get out of their way to help them learn about their own learning.

Sharing student projects beyond the walls of the school is the ultimate goal. By publishing beyond the school, students present their work to an authentic audience for meaningful feedback.

Using Digital Tools for Storytelling

The ancient art of storytelling is practiced in many different ways in classrooms across all content areas and grade levels. When this art employs technology, students can create and broadcast their work to a global audience by publishing their stories on a variety of platforms, including Twitter, Facebook, blogs, wikis, YouTube, screen-sharing websites, LMSs, and videoconferences.

Students use all different types of technology, including cell phones, digital cameras, editing software, drones outfitted with cameras, moviemaking software, and YouTube, for digital storytelling. The rapid advance of technology has dramatically simplified the process of creating a digital story. The tools continually become less complicated and easier to use; and in many cases, the entire process can be completed for little money or even for free. Before jumping to the use of the tools, it is important to review what makes a story compelling to an audience.

Importance of a Good Story

To create a compelling story, students must become digital storytellers. They must understand the elements of planning, storyboarding, collaborating, recording videos, photographing, video editing, audio editing, telling stories, and publishing. Although these sound technically complicated, the process can be initiated in the classroom with the simple question, What should my story be about?

A compelling story is one that captures and engages an audience through images and sound. A series of pictures and music is nothing more than a slideshow. A digital storyteller weaves the images, video, and sound together to tell an interesting narrative. Most classroom projects only require a slideshow with music, but with practice, even very young students can create stories that capture audiences of all ages.

Planning is the key to successful digital storytelling. Too often, students report to the computer lab and start creating a story without preplanning. The process must include offline planning, collaborating, and visualizing the story before reaching for the camera or keyboard. Learning the digital storytelling process in small groups helps with classroom management. It allows teachers to troubleshoot technical issues and students to help support other learners at different levels. Start with simple digital stories and build the complexity, keeping the focus on telling a powerful story, not the technology tools students use to tell it.

Sharing the assessment rubric with students before the planning begins keeps them focused during the entire process. Visit Kathy Schrock's comprehensive website (www.schrockguide.net/digital-storytelling.html) for sample rubrics.

Storyboards

Start with a storyboard to help students visualize the entire story instead of focusing on specific shots or story elements. A *storyboard* is a visual representation of the story the student plans on creating. Hollywood directors need very sophisticated storyboards to create a movie; students' storyboards need not be that complex. To create storyboards, students can use index cards, sticky notes, or any small pieces of paper that they can shuffle. If students can access technology, another way to create a storyboard is through presentation software such as PowerPoint, Keynote, the app and website Haiku Deck, or Google Slides.

Planning with presentation software simplifies the digital storytelling process by keeping the focus on the story before jumping to technology tools, apps, or websites. The selection of technology tools for creating the final project should come after students have crafted the story. Planning ahead greatly simplifies the production and editing process, saving time in the long run. In addition, learning how to collaborate during planning is an essential skill students need for life and work outside of school.

Using the Slide Sorter view in PowerPoint (an overall view of slide thumbnail images), students can sequence concepts and big ideas on the slides and add details during the planning process. As the story unfolds, they can rearrange, delete, or clarify parts of the story. Groups of students can work around one computer, or students can work individually. In the case of Google Slides, they can share the project with the group, and everyone can access the same presentation in real time from any Internet-enabled device inside or outside of school.

Collaborating in the Cloud

Collaborating in the cloud is a relatively new concept. The term *the cloud* means accessing the Internet, anytime, anywhere, from any device, for free, and with collaboration by multiple users possible. Google Drive is the best example for collaborating in the cloud. For example, after logging into Google Drive, a student creates a presentation and shares the document with the group. Each member can contribute, edit, and work from any device that is connected to the Internet. Everyone can participate and work in real time; that is the beauty of collaborating in the cloud.

Before the cloud, users had to save files to a hard drive or server, where only one person at a time could open and use them. If a group shared multiple copies of the file, someone had to manually merge the edits from each copy into one document. The cloud eliminates the merging process because there are no *copies* of the document; everyone on the project works on the same document in real time from anywhere, and users can see the edits of others as they occur. This is the reality in the majority of our colleges and universities, and we need to help students be ready to be productive in the cloud.

Project Assessment

Once the group agrees that the storyboard is complete, it should submit the document to the teacher for approval before moving into project creation. The teacher and group should confer, using the established rubric, to evaluate the group storyboard. When the teacher takes the time to give specific feedback to groups at this point, it helps streamline the production process as well as keep the focus on the story. Students need ongoing and seamless assessment feedback throughout the digital storytelling process. Assessing a digital story can be complicated if the teacher does not establish and clarify expectations before the planning process begins. Assessment expectations should be specific yet flexible enough to allow groups to craft their stories clearly and produce them using a variety of technology tools. Figure 2.1 is an example of a rubric I used for a third-grade class. The assignment was to use some type of technology to create a public service announcement about preventing bullying. Each group selected its own technology tool, and I asked students to act out part of the video and also add some audio.

	Content	Performance	Technical
1	I love it and want to watch it again! It is very informative. It is easy to understand. It shows understanding of the topic.	It shows great enthusiasm. The pace is not too fast or too slow. The audio supports the message. Practice is evident.	Technology tool helps create a quality product. The audio is clear and easy to understand.
2	It keeps my attention. It is mostly informative. I understood most of it. It shows moderate understanding of the topic.	It shows some enthusiasm. The pace needs a little work. The audio is not clear. It needs more practice.	Technology tool could be used in a better way. The audio distracts from the message.
3	It is kind of boring. It is somewhat informative. Parts are understandable. It shows some understanding of the topic.	It lacks enthusiasm. The pace needs some work. The audio is very hard to understand. Some practice is evident.	Technology tool distracts from the message. The audio is incomplete.
4	It is very dull! It lacks information. It is hard to follow. It shows little understanding of the topic.	It is boring! It is much too slow or too fast. There is no audio. No practice is evident.	No technology is used. No audio track is used.

Figure 2.1: Third-grade rubric for public service announcement.

Including Digital Images in Projects

When students create nonlinguistic representation projects, chances are they will have to collect digital images. Images help students understand vocabulary, concepts, relationships, and context around topics. They can provide the hook students need to help remember concepts and processes. In this section, you will learn how to use students' images, collect images online, and edit images to enhance projects.

Image Use for Projects

The easiest images to use in projects are those students draw or take using a digital device, because then there is no concern about copyright infringement. Students can scan the images they draw and convert them into digital objects or use a device with a camera to snap a picture of the drawing. Students can even draw using their computers or tablets. Some tablet computers even have swivel screens and a stylus, simplifying the drawing process.

Students can create and archive their own original illustrations with Google Drive's drawing feature. Students can draw using any Internet-enabled device, but this process can be tricky with a mouse or trackpad. Using a stylus to draw on a tablet or other device is much easier. Students can save the resulting images as graphics and incorporate them into their projects.

Most schools have policies about using images of students, which teachers must be careful to follow. In some schools, parents or guardians sign a release for the use of their students' images. Teachers should make sure they know exactly who is on the do-not-photograph list, especially if students share their projects outside of school. Within these rules, teachers can snap pictures of students working on projects, artwork on the bulletin boards, science projects, or school events. Teachers can use these images for student projects, curriculum night presentations, and as an archive to share instructional practices.

Organizing the digital images is another challenge. The device that collects the images determines how they're organized. Several applications have made it easy to share and send images to other devices. Dropbox is one answer for student groups needing to send their files to one computer or tablet.

Image Collection Online

The Internet can be a rich source of images. Countless websites store and organize all types of images. However, it is critical that teachers and students understand basic copyright laws before using images in projects. Just because an image is posted online doesn't mean it is copyright free. My classroom rule was only to use images with the Creative Commons permissions, and every image had to be cited by copying the link to the page where I found the image. When companies or individual users publish a photo online, they assign it copyright permissions. For example, when publishing an image to a website, the user selects among the following permissions.

- **Copyrighted, all rights reserved:** The person or group who uploaded this image has reserved all the rights. People should not use these images without getting written permission from the photographer.

- **Creative Commons free to use and share noncommercially:** People can use these images, but they can't modify the images.

- **Creative Commons free to use and share, even commercially:** People can use these images, even if they sell what they created.

- **Creative Commons free to use, share, or modify noncommercially:** This Creative Commons designation means that people can use and modify the images privately, but they cannot use them if the product is sold commercially.

- **Creative Commons free to use, share, or modify, even commercially:** Although the images are free to use, people should still cite the source of each image they use (Creative Commons, n.d.).

Teachers should direct students to search for images that are licensed under Creative Commons or that are free to share. They should also teach students how to cite images to give appropriate credit to the owner. Both teachers and students can use images, cited properly, in their projects. It's essential to teach students about copyright issues and share them with colleagues in order to model the ethical use of digital media.

Google Docs has a research tool built in that automatically cites any image added to the document, if the student searches in the search box that appears to the right on the screen. In Google Docs, Slides, and Drawings, under the tools menu, students select *research* to open the search. When the student places the image in his or her document, a citation is automatically added to the bottom of the page. Right within the document, the student can select the usage rights as well as the citation formats of MLA, APA, and Chicago.

Many image databases can be found online. Most large websites have an advanced search option to eliminate any images that are not licensed under Creative Commons. I prefer Flickr to search for images because of its advanced search feature (www.flickr.com/search/advanced). Google Images also has an advanced search feature for those who prefer it (https://images.google.com/advanced_search). Once you have located the appropriate image for a project, download and save the image into a folder on the computer or device.

Sites for Copyright-Friendly Images

- Pics4Learning (www.pics4learning.com) is a copyright-friendly image library for teachers and students.

- Stockvault (www.stockvault.net) offers free stock photos for personal, noncommercial use.

- The Library of Congress (http://memory.loc.gov/ammem/index.html) has some images that are okay to use. Check each collection for copyright information.

- In the NASA image gallery (http://nix.nasa.gov), most images are not copyrighted.

- The NOAA photo library (www.photolib.noaa.gov) also has great images that are free to use.

Image-generator websites and apps are another source for finding and creating images. They provide the image and then allow you to add your own text, which becomes part of the image. For example, on the website ImageChef (www.imagechef .com), there is an image of alphabet soup, and users add a message, which looks like it is floating in the soup. This site offers a great way to create thematic vocabulary words, quick greetings, or presentation slides. One caution is that some of the images are not appropriate for younger students.

Image Editing for Projects

My favorite iPad app for generating images is PixyMe (www.pixyme.com), which is located in the iTunes store. The app has a large collection of bold, colorful, and contemporary images and is updated frequently. This company uses the term *image personalization*.

Editing images used to require expensive software and specific training, but today, many free and low-cost image-editing software options, apps, and websites are available to choose from. One free app on Apple and Android devices is Pixlr (https:// pixlr.com). It has a wide range of editing options, effects, overlays, borders, and much more. The free Picasa software from Google (http://picasa.google.com) is loaded with features for editing and sharing images online. Users can download the feature-rich software to their computers. Adobe Photoshop Elements (www.adobe.com/products /photoshop-elements.html) offers more advanced editing options. This is a limited version of Photoshop that is easy to use yet powerful. Look for the free download trial and education pricing.

Creating Video Projects

Reading, writing, and speaking should be part of every class across all subject areas. One common classroom project that incorporates all three skills is to create a newscast on any of various topics. By using different digital tools, students can take this project to the redefinition stage of the SAMR model. As mentioned previously, the SAMR model moves lessons from linguistic pencil-and-paper tasks to higher-order, richer products that students can share with an authentic audience. Let's take this example through each step of the model.

1. **Substitution:** Students type a script for their newscasts instead of writing the scripts using pencil and paper.

2. **Augmentation:** Students collect digital images to show during the various news segments.

3. **Modification:** Students use a smartphone or digital camera to record classroom broadcasts.

4. **Redefinition:** Students broadcast their newscast to a live audience using a teleprompter app that scrolls the script. They connect with an authentic audience using Skype (www.skype.com/en) or Ustream (www.ustream.tv) while videotaping each segment. When they complete the recording, groups post the video to the class YouTube channel. During the presentation, students observing the newscast monitor the backchannel to answer audience questions using TodaysMeet (https://todaysmeet.com). The teacher tweets a link to the class YouTube channel. This is a good example of how a video lesson can get out the door to a broader audience.

Videos are everywhere on the web today, and creating them is easier than ever. This no longer requires expensive software and equipment. Today, so many apps, websites, and software tools are available that even very young children can use them to create amazing video presentations. Five of the many countless options for creating videos are highlighted here.

iMovie

The first option for creating videos is iMovie (www.apple.com/mac/imovie), which comes as free software on Apple computers or as an app on an iPhone or iPad. Robust and powerful, iMovie can create long, complex videos or quick movie trailers on any topic imaginable.

Animoto

The second option is Animoto (https://animoto.com). This is a free service that gives the user many different options, including backgrounds, image libraries, and a good selection of royalty-free music. After the user finishes dragging and dropping images and video clips, Animoto hosts the final video on its website. The presentations look professional thanks to the many templates and music options. Educators can navigate to https://animoto.com/education/classroom to apply for a free Animoto Plus account and access to additional features.

WeVideo

The third option is WeVideo (www.wevideo.com), another free online service that makes it possible to create and edit videos from any Internet-connected device without the need to install software. The feature-rich website allows users to produce stunning video projects, share videos with their team, and edit them in real time. Connect WeVideo as an app through Google Drive to get the best storage options.

Do Ink

The fourth option, Do Ink (www.doink.com), is an iPad app that is very popular with elementary teachers. This app makes it possible to create animations, work with graphics, and create short videos. Users now have the ability to create videos using chroma key technology, which is often called the green-screen or blue-screen method. Simplified, this means that a student is videotaped in front of a blue or green screen, and then another image is placed in the background, making it look as if there has been a change of scenery.

YouTube

Finally, YouTube (www.youtube.com) has features to customize and publish videos. Once logged in with a Google account on YouTube, users click on the Upload button to open the various features. The slideshow creator makes it possible to create quick yet professional-looking slideshows, and there is a large collection of royalty-free music to select from. There is also a video editor to trim and crop videos. The final project is published to YouTube.

Creating Podcasts and Audio Projects

Video projects can be fun for students of all ages, but creating an audio presentation, like a radio talk show, is another option with fewer factors to consider. An online audio file is also called a podcast. There are hundreds of thousands of podcasts floating around the Internet, but the largest organized collection is in the iTunes Store (www .apple.com/itunes). Podcasts come in all shapes and sizes; some are only a few minutes long, while others go on for hours. The topics range from college lectures to hobbies and everything else in between. Search iTunes to get a sense of the many available podcasts. In the classroom, students can create their own podcasts as a nonlinguistic representation of something they have learned.

Students can record podcasts on several different devices. Any device with a built-in microphone works for this purpose. Students also can use an external microphone to record themselves reading, interviewing each other, or acting out a scene from a book. They can even use the sound recorder on a computer to create a very simple podcast. Cell phones have a voice recorder and can provide a quick way to get started with podcasts. There are many free websites with which to create and share podcasts. One website that is quick and easy to use is PodOmatic (www.podomatic.com). Another website for creating and publishing podcasts is Podbean (www.podbean.com).

Users also can use special software to create and edit podcasts. A popular option for Macs and PCs is the free software Audacity (http://audacity.sourceforge.net), and Macs also offer GarageBand (www.apple.com/mac/garageband). These software options allow users to both edit audio clips and add music to any part of the clip. GarageBand enables users, even novices, to compose music. Students who enjoy creating podcasts will quickly move beyond the basic, free websites and look for software like these to edit their work.

Similar to images, large databases of sound clips and musical selections are available online. Many websites offer free clips with the option to subscribe for more clips. It is important to model the ethical use of all digital resources, including music and audio clips, and explain to students the consequences of failing to respect copyright law. For example, if a student uses copyrighted music in a presentation without the permission of the owner, and then he or she publishes the project to YouTube, when the file is scanned and matched against a large database of copyrighted music, YouTube will reject the project.

Websites for Audio Clips and Music

- www.royaltyfreemusic.com
- http://incompetech.com/music/royalty-free
- www.mobygratis.com

Once students learn the basics of podcasting, they can select this option for individual or group projects. Having students record podcasts at different intervals during the year is a good way to track fluency progress. Podcasts in other languages can even allow some students to communicate with parents in their native languages.

Publishing Student Projects Online

After students create their nonlinguistic representations, publishing is the next step. Videos can be shared internally through email or an LMS. To get the projects out to a broader audience, students can publish their projects online to sites such as YouTube (www.youtube.com) or Vimeo (https://vimeo.com). Students like to publish and keep track of how many times their work is viewed.

Restructuring Research Using the SAMR Model

Research is a part of almost every class. Try restructuring your next research project using the SAMR model. Consider student choice and small-group projects using nonlinguistic representations. The following is an example of how you can use the SAMR model for a research project.

Substitution: Students research a topic using a chosen search engine.

Augmentation: Students collect digital images and organize the images into folders.

Modification: Students sequence their information and images using presentation software such as PowerPoint or Google Slides.

Redefinition: Groups of students gather research and images about the topic and create a thirty-second trailer about it. Each group selects the technology tool that it will use to create the video. Some options might include iMovie, Animoto, Do Ink, or WeVideo. When group members complete the project, they upload it to the class YouTube channel and share the link through social media, inviting others to post comments for each presentation.

To publish student work to YouTube, teachers can create a class playlist on their free YouTube channel. The teacher selects to allow comments for the video, opening students to feedback beyond the walls of the classroom. Opening comments on student work could invite outsiders to comment as well, so everyone needs to understand that negative comments are a possibility. Most teachers who are publishing student work also are teaching students how to react to potential negative comments. The good news is that teachers who manage a YouTube channel can remove comments.

I encourage teachers to allow comments, which can help students learn how to be responsible digital citizens by publishing thoughtful comments. Students love the authentic feedback and the interaction with others. Also, be prepared for students to compare the number of comments and hits with each other. YouTube has many analytical tools students are likely interested in exploring.

Using digital images, audio, music, and videos to create nonlinguistic representations provides students with opportunities for deeper learning as well as a valuable skill set for future success. The experience of planning, creating, building, refining, and sharing their projects beyond classroom walls is important for student development and achievement.

◢◤ Team Discussion Questions

Use the following questions for personal review, professional development, or as a discussion guide for collaborative groups in your PLC.

1. Before reading chapter 2, what did the phrase *nonlinguistic representation* mean to you? After reading the chapter, how would you explain the idea to a colleague?

2. In your current practice, how do you, or would you like to, use nonlinguistic representations with students?

3. What is your previous experience in creating videos, and what did you learn about the process?

4. Although there are countless platforms, apps, and software solutions available for creating videos, only a few are highlighted in this chapter. Which application do you plan on trying first, and why?

5. Planning for a digital story using presentation software is a strategy shared in this chapter as a technology alternative to pencil and paper. Compare and contrast the two planning approaches.

6. What does it mean if an image is licensed under Creative Commons?

7. What did you learn about copyright as it relates to using digital images, and how will you disseminate this information to your students?

8. Several databases for collecting digital images are mentioned in this chapter. Which collection do you plan on exploring first?

9. *Cloud computing* is a confusing concept for many people. Please write a short paragraph to explain this idea to someone who has never heard the phrase.

10. When working with digital images, you often need to edit them. Of the websites and apps mentioned in this chapter, which one do you plan on exploring first, and why?

CHAPTER 3

Using Technology Tools for Formative Evaluation

Creating multimedia projects and publishing the work for a global audience is an excellent way to increase learning for a wider group of students. However, it poses a new set of challenges in terms of formative evaluation. This chapter introduces strategies to provide quality formative evaluation using technology tools, websites, apps, and more in the classroom and beyond.

Technology constantly changes; new tools appear and favorites disappear every day. So while I discuss particular tools in this chapter, the real goal is to help teachers build a toolkit of formative evaluation tools. Teachers can then mix up these tools as they gather critical feedback from students during the learning process instead of waiting for the final summative test after the unit is complete.

In my role as instructional coach, I worked with a particularly talented fifth-grade teacher. Sandra is always ready and willing to try any new thing that comes along. Sandra has designed her class as a teacher-student partnership, with the students directing much of their learning. On one visit, I found Sandra's science classroom buzzing with groups independently researching systems of the human body. Part of the task for each group was to design five assessment questions for the rest of the class to answer after the group presentation. In addition to creating the questions, groups had to decide which formative evaluation technology tool they would use to present the questions and how they planned to share the data they gathered with the teacher.

I thought this was a big task for fifth-grade students but soon discovered that they had brainstormed some of the formative assessment tools they had already used. I was not surprised to see Kahoot! at the top of the list, followed by Socrative, Google Forms, and Poll Everywhere. I asked Sandra about adding Plickers (www.plickers.com)

to the list, and Sandra wrote a couple of sample questions on the Plickers website. She then added the students' names with accompanying numbers, while I gathered the paper cards we printed off the Plickers website. From the website, you can print up to forty-eight unique cards with symbols that coordinate with student numbers. Every card lists A, B, C, and D on each side.

We gave each student a piece of paper with the number from the Plickers website that coordinated with his or her name. Next, we displayed the multiple-choice or true/false questions on a large screen. Students then picked up their papers and turned them to reflect the answer to each question (A, B, C, or D). Sandra used the app on her smartphone to scan the room, automatically recording, color-coding, and charting student responses right on her phone!

The use of Plickers is difficult to explain because it seems impossible to collect information from students based on how they hold up a piece of paper. However, this is how it works, and Sandra immediately had the information on her smartphone. We asked the students what they thought after they answered a few questions, and we all laughed when one of her students said it was magic!

Wow! Seeing this app in action excited everyone in the room. Immediately, students wanted to answer more questions, and we had a lively discussion about how the technology worked. After a few more questions and scans, the conversation shifted to comparing and contrasting the different formative assessment tools we had worked with. I was shocked when these fifth graders discussed features of the various apps and websites and how Plickers could fit into the toolkit of resources they could use for their assessments after the presentations. One boy pointed out that Plickers would be a great choice for the following week because most of their computers were being pulled for use during testing (S. Raymond, personal communication, August 4, 2014). Formative assessment data using one phone and some pieces of paper—I can't wait to see the next great thing!

Many websites are moving into the formative evaluation arena, offering different services and new ways to engage students during lessons. Some of these solutions are in a game-show-type format, while others allow students to draw a picture as an answer. Included in this chapter are a wide variety of solutions teachers can use to provide critical feedback to students. Technology tools can provide quick checks of student knowledge or learning before, during, and after the lesson. This chapter helps teachers gather a virtual toolkit of formative assessment tools.

Before we dive into the tools, we should have a common understanding of the term *formative evaluation*. On their resource-rich website Visible Learning (http://visible-learning.org), John Hattie and his team define *formative evaluation* as:

> Any activity used as an assessment of learning progress before
> or during the learning process itself. In contrast with formative as-
> sessment, the summative assessment evaluates what students
> know or have learned at the end of the teaching, after all is done.
> (Visible Learning, 2015)

I follow Hattie's distinction of formative evaluation and summative assessment. This chapter focuses on formative evaluation during the learning process using technology tools and platforms—specifically, apps, software, devices, and other platforms for teachers and students to use while learning inside and outside of the classroom.

Exploring Formative Evaluation Technology

Historically, formative evaluation tools, such as classroom audience response systems or classroom clickers, have been very expensive and limited. The clicker devices come in class sets. This device resembles a remote control with a variety of options for answering questions the teacher creates. Each student uses an ID code to log in to the clicker. The teacher creates higher-order questions for formative evaluation, and once he or she launches the software, students can submit their answers. The teacher then reveals the answers. He or she can use the data for clarification and discussion. The results displayed through the projector reflect the answers from the class as a whole rather than from individual students. The projector displays no student names or ID numbers; however, after the lesson, the teacher can drill down into the spreadsheet the program creates. Some devices have a self-study mode, allowing students to work through a quiz at their own pace rather than through teacher-directed responses.

At the writing of this book, classroom sets (including devices, software, and transponder) range in cost from about $1,500 to $2,000 per classroom. The system works very well when the teacher has adequately prepared through professional development and set up the hardware and software correctly, and when students are accustomed to using the devices.

The purpose of the investment is to engage every student in the evaluation, and when used properly, it is effective. Unfortunately, this is not always the case. In many schools, this technology ends up locked in storerooms instead of in the hands of students because someone did not install or update the software correctly, leading to frustration. So although some still use the clickers, there is a movement toward different technology solutions.

Alternative formative evaluation tools, apps, websites, and devices have appeared online, and many of them are free. These new applications are often more intuitive for both teachers and students. Data can be collected from any Internet-enabled device. Every student could have a different device in his or her hands and still participate in the same evaluation. This option is particularly helpful for the many schools across the globe that have moved to the bring-your-own-device or technology system, often referred to as BYOD or BYOT.

A longtime leader in online formative assessment and evaluation is Socrative (http://socrative.com). On this website, the teacher creates an account and receives a code for each class. He or she can then create a quiz of multiple-choice or true/false questions on the website. Students can use any Internet-enabled device to answer the questions.

While students are working, the teacher can privately watch live results on the website. Socrative has a number of options, including hiding student names, randomizing the question order, and allowing student feedback during the assessment. The teacher can generate class and individual student results after the assessment in the form of a spreadsheet. Socrative is a popular website among teachers for this type of formative evaluation.

> The previous chapter focused on nonlinguistic representations and mentioned that students can generate and archive original drawings using the Google Drive drawing feature. Students can submit their illustrations to the teacher using an LMS like Google Classroom. The teacher can use the drawings for a class discussion or formative evaluation and save the work of individual students.

Google Forms, within the Google Drive suite (https://drive.google.com), is a powerful tool for formative evaluation. Teachers create forms and ask students to complete them online. While students complete the forms, teachers can observe the results on the companion spreadsheet. Teachers can then use the data to identify students who could benefit from further instruction on the material. Google Forms includes the ability to customize themes and insert images and videos into the material. For example, a teacher could create an interest inventory for students by writing a series of questions each student will answer independently. The students can use any Internet-enabled device to access the form and answer the questions. Teachers also can use forms to collect data from colleagues about upcoming events, professional development, and data from PLC meetings.

The particular website or app is not important. The formative evaluation data and the way teachers and students use the information for teaching and learning are the real focus. Accessible and usable data are far more important than the features of particular websites and apps. Data, however informative, that teachers cannot export into an easily manipulated and archived format are of limited use. Fortunately, most of the formative assessment websites allow teachers to display student data in a spreadsheet, making them easier to compare, contrast, and use. The tasks teachers ask students to complete should help them become lifelong learners. Students will continue to encounter formative evaluations, both formal and informal, in higher education as well as the workplace; therefore, educators must prepare students to meet these expectations.

Organizing and Managing Evaluations

Organizing feedback, reflections, and evaluations throughout the year can be challenging in any busy classroom environment. If handheld technology is available to teachers, they can use devices to capture and organize formative evaluation feedback from students. Depending on the availability of these devices, the teacher can use voice memos, video clips, digital pictures, typed text, or handwritten notes for data collection. The system the teacher creates to organize these data depends on the available technology and connectivity to the Internet.

Google Drive is a good option for storing artifacts and organizing ongoing reflections. Reflections on instructional practice should be part of the teaching and learning process, but organizing the reflections can be a challenge for busy educators. The best way to stay organized within Google Drive is to create one folder for each student and then develop a naming system to use for all documents, for example, "last name_class period_brief description_date" (that is, Ormiston_2_imageofexperiment_12-15). Starting the system with a good file structure and naming conventions saves time and streamlines the reporting of information that teachers gather throughout the formative evaluation process.

Two other platforms for organizing information into one consistent system are Evernote and Microsoft OneNote. Users can organize information through their websites or their apps.

Evernote (https://evernote.com) has a different look and feel than Google Drive, more like a traditional notebook. It is an app for smartphones linked to an online website. Once the user creates a free account, downloads the app, and creates a notebook, Evernote automatically syncs every notebook entry between the website and the app. The user interface is simple yet robust, and with an upgrade to the premium version, additional options become available, including sharing and discussing ideas with anyone in the world, annotating PDFs, scanning business cards, clipping and organizing information from any website, turning notes into presentations, and gaining offline access.

Microsoft OneNote (www.onenote.com), like Evernote, allows teachers to create notebooks and share them with others. OneNote works on Macs as well as PCs. See

Microsoft OneNote in the Classroom (Microsoft, 2015) to learn more about classroom uses of OneNote.

Capturing and Recording Student Interactions

Recording student interactions is another way to gather evaluation feedback. Audio recordings allow teachers to capture dynamic in-class discussions. This is a great way to gather ideas from students who might have a print-based disability. (Chapter 2's section Creating Podcasts and Audio Projects helps teachers create a system for capturing audio files.) Teachers can share these recordings with an authentic audience outside the classroom by publishing the audio files to blogs, wikis, or websites.

Many free websites and apps also record audio for assessment purposes. Several options are available, but a good place to start is the website VoiceThread (http://voicethread.com), because the interface is easy to use and sharing is simplified. Students plan and then record their audio segments on the VoiceThread website or app and then invite other people to listen to their podcasts and leave comments using a webcam, text, or audio. This website simplifies the process of recording and publishing as well as gathering feedback from an authentic audience.

One of my favorite apps for recording and sharing student-created audio clips is AudioNote (available through iTunes). This app comes with a five-dollar price tag and is only available on iPads or iPhones. The app is well worth the money because during playback, teacher lessons and student-typed text are highlighted and saved in a video format that can be viewed through a free app. AudioNote is a great way for the teacher to observe how students are processing the lesson and provide feedback as formative evaluation. A feature on AudioNote allows the user to upload a video to Google Drive to simplify viewing and sharing the video file. This feature and many others are helpful for students of all ages and abilities.

As mentioned in chapter 1, Kaizena is an app for Google Drive that enables the use of audio comments in a Google Doc. The teacher embeds the audio clip into the Google Doc, making it possible for students to receive feedback when they open the document at home or school. The teacher can use this feedback during the teaching and learning process for formative evaluation instead of waiting until the final project is submitted and assigning a grade as a summative assessment. Think of Kaizena as a way to provide ongoing formative evaluation during document creation.

Collaborating Using Technology

Teachers should invite students to participate in the formative evaluation process instead of waiting for the final summative assessment grade and feedback after work is completed. Involvement in ongoing evaluation will be new to most students, but understanding the process will help them see how evaluation can occur not just after the assignment is submitted but also during the learning process. All feedback does not need to flow just from teacher to student. With the use of collaborative features of technology tools, students will quickly learn how to adjust their work based on ongoing feedback.

Groups of students can collaborate on a report, project, or notes inside and outside of school on any Internet-enabled device. For instance, Google Slides, unlike Microsoft PowerPoint, makes it possible for students to edit and collaborate in real time during a presentation. To engage students during the lesson, the teacher first shares the Google Slides presentation with the class. Each student makes a copy and saves it to his or her individual Google Drive. During the teacher's presentation, students take notes on their own devices in the Speaker Notes section. Google Slides associates the students' notes with the teacher's presentation slides, making it easier to study for assessments. When students make a copy of the presentation, their notes are saved on Google Drive.

Technology should not create more work for teachers. Fortunately, teachers who already have prepared lessons using software like Microsoft PowerPoint or Keynote by Apple can upload their presentations to Google Drive to enable real-time collaboration. The teacher can open the presentations using the Google Drive viewer, which converts the presentation to a Google Slides presentation that can be shared with students. The downside to this is that formatting does not always convert perfectly, so some adjustments might be needed, specifically to fonts, images, and alignment.

The scale of the transition to digital collaboration became evident in a strategic planning meeting I attended in October 2014 at a regional career tech center for all the county high schools. This was the first time this group of twenty professionals had come together to plan for the future of a career and tech education (CTE) center.

Around the conference table were high school students, business leaders, high school CTE teachers, building administrators, and higher education faculty. The principal of the career center facilitating the meeting asked everyone to brainstorm specific topics by recording ideas in a Google Doc. The principal had the Google Doc projected on the screen for the group to see, and the same document was also on the computer in front of every

continued →

participant. For the majority of the people around the table, including the principal, this was their first exposure to using a Google Doc for collaborative work in real time.

At first, a few brave people typed into the document, while the others sat back and watched, unsure of how to participate. As the meeting progressed, more people joined in the process, but clearly some people were uncomfortable putting their ideas into the document. By capturing the ideas in one section, it was easier for the group to move to the next part of the process—goal setting. It was a challenge for the principal to facilitate the large group and record ideas at the same time. As the meeting progressed, more team members jumped in and helped with recording and editing.

The building secretary was at the table, furiously taking notes with a pad of paper and a pen. As I observed this process, I thought about how difficult it is to change people's habits. I am sure the secretary is a whiz at the computer keyboard, but her mindset was still to grab a paper and a pen for a meeting.

The principal tried a new way to communicate by modeling the use of Google Docs for the group. It is important to recognize that this type of collaboration takes time and practice for adults too. Introducing new technology and processes can be a challenge, but through patience and practice, the process becomes smoother.

My schedule made it impossible for me to be at the conference table for the second meeting. From hundreds of miles away, I still participated in the planning process by contributing ideas, adding my comments into the shared document. This type of modeling and process change only happens when school leaders take risks and demonstrate that they are also learners.

Collaborative Note Taking

Effective note taking is a critical college and career skill that every student must master to be successful inside and outside of the classroom. Taking notes using paper is a different process than taking notes using a computer, phone, or tablet. People of all ages can have trouble giving up physical notebooks in favor of digital notebooks. While no one should force technology on people who prefer paper, many willingly adopt the technology route given enough time and practice.

Students must learn how to create a note-taking system for recording, reflecting on, and organizing information using paper and pencil or accessible technology tools inside and outside of the classroom, as it is critical for their success. Educators may wish to design a standard organizational system for each grade level or the whole building.

Students can collaborate to take notes if they have access to devices during the lesson. Those who are strong note takers can model for other students how to organize notes and capture the key topics during the lesson. Students who struggle with structuring ideas can see effective note taking in action. This strategy may not work for some students because of their learning styles, but it can help struggling students, students out of class, and students with certain disabilities.

Collaborative note taking is one way students can prepare for an assessment, but they also need strategies to review the notes and identify critical information for study, such as color-coding key vocabulary words or topics. Highlighting key text and using different fonts creatively are other options. Within the Google Drive environment, students and teachers can use the Comments feature to clarify key topics as they study. If students take notes individually, they can work in collaborative groups to review the notes each person recorded and create their own collaborative study guide before the assessment.

Shared note taking might seem like cheating to some teachers, but the world outside of school views this type of activity as collaboration. Using technology, people who can't attend the meeting or class in person can still participate, contributing ideas from anywhere in the world.

Successful Pencasts

For those learners who need a pen in their hands to take notes, the Livescribe Smartpen (www.livescribe.com) is a remarkable piece of technology to streamline note taking. The pen is paired with specialized notebooks, and as the teacher teaches, the student using the Smartpen creates a *pencast* of the lesson. The pen syncs what the teacher is saying to the notes the student is writing. The lesson is then saved as a video to be used for review. These videos can be shared with other people as well.

The pens and notebook packs do come with a hefty price tag. Some of the earlier versions are available on various websites at a much lower cost. Some third-party apps also work with the pens. Reflecting back to the strategic planning meeting earlier in the chapter, if the secretary had used this Smartpen, her notes would have automatically become digital.

Using Blogs and Wikis

The collaborative creation of a document is just one step of the process. Next is publishing using blogs and wikis. This supports formative evaluation because most blogs and wikis are considered works in progress, not polished, edited, complex writing pieces. Using blog and wiki platforms, students can collect suggestions, edits, and comments throughout the learning process. Questions from others can help students focus and craft their writing during formative assessment—before the writing is complete and published. Think of blogs and wikis as works in progress versus final published products. The use of blog and wiki platforms takes practice, and both students and teachers should allow themselves time to explore what works.

The process of *blogging* is best described as creating an online journal and making that journal public. In education, the three biggest blog platforms are Blogger (www .blogger.com), Edublogs (http://edublogs.org), and Kidblog (http://kidblog.org). Kidblog and Edublogs are the most user friendly, allowing teachers to quickly set up a class blog as well as individual student blogs. Kidblog has some nice templates for elementary teachers, while most teachers in middle school and high school seem to prefer the look and feel of Edublogs.

Blogs are usually individual endeavors, whereas a wiki is more like a public shared Google Doc about a certain topic. Wikis were used extensively before Google Drive became so common in schools. The two websites most educators use to create wikis are Wikispaces (www.wikispaces.com) and PBWorks (www.pbworks.com).

Before setting up a classroom blog, teachers should check with administrators about using students' names and the need to seek parents' permission before posting student work. Most teachers set up a classroom blog for general information, and then each student has his or her own blog page linked to the main page.

The teacher must be diligent about moderating comments for student work. Blog settings should require that the teacher approves all comments before they appear on students' pages. This is an important precaution to protect students from unwanted or negative comments.

Once the teacher has set up the blogging environment and administrators have approved it, students can start writing and posting to the blog. Some teachers post blog assignments on the main class blog, while others allow students to use their blogs without giving specific assignments.

Digital images make blog posts more interesting, but teachers should make sure everyone understands the school policy before anyone posts pictures of other students. Including a picture of the student on his or her individual blog may not be a good idea, but the teacher could encourage students to post pictures of art projects they have created to add interest to their blog posts.

The purpose of creating a class blog or wiki is to get students writing to a broader, authentic audience. Comments from other people inside and outside the classroom can motivate many bloggers. Learning how to write good comments on a blog takes instruction and practice. Teachers should model what good comments look like, and then have students practice by commenting on classmates' blog posts.

Once students have created a few blog posts and practiced commenting, it's time to get the work out to a broader audience. To get started, a teacher might share the link to the blog or blogs of his or her students with other teachers and students in the school, inviting comments and feedback. The teacher could also invite families and friends nearby and across the globe, encouraging them to comment on student work.

Social media is another way to reach a broader audience. For teachers on Twitter, it is simple to tweet the link to the class blog and include the hashtag for the school district, if there is one, as well as the hashtag #comments4kids. This hashtag is a group that many people follow to provide specific feedback for student projects and writing. Many blogging platforms include a map that shows where in the world people are reading the blog; this motivates students, encouraging them to continue writing.

SAMR Writing Blog Example

A primary school teacher gave students the task of building a model and then writing about what they created. The following SAMR example transforms this task from a pencil-and-paper activity to a project shared with a broader audience.

Substitution: Instead of writing the sentences on paper, students type their sentences on a computer or tablet.

Augmentation: Students use the spell-check feature in the word processing software to check their spelling.

Modification: Students take digital pictures of their models and insert the images into the text they have written.

Redefinition: Students create the model and then take digital pictures, type their sentences, and publish them on their class blog. The teacher tweets messages to invite others to comment on student work. Students read and respond to the comments from other students across the globe.

Designing Exit Slip Activities

There are countless ways to gather formative evaluation feedback in the form of exit slip activities using a pencil and paper. The premise of the strategy is basically this: in the last few minutes of class, the teacher asks a higher-order question about the lesson. Before students can exit the classroom, they submit slips of paper with their answers to the teacher. Collecting last-minute data for formative evaluation helps both students and teachers summarize the lesson.

Technology streamlines the process of collecting and organizing data. By making this process more efficient, the teacher has more time to study the data collected and modify instruction and pacing as needed. Skip the paper if students have Internet-enabled devices or smartphones with which to participate.

A variety of apps, software, and websites allow teachers to collect these data quickly and compile the information into a spreadsheet. The teacher can then look at the class as a whole group and also drill into the results of individual students to discover trends and patterns. Following are examples of specific, quick exit slip activities using various technologies.

Three-Word Summary Using a Google Form

Visualizing a three-word summary is a modification of an instructional strategy that often employs small slips of paper or sticky notes. In the traditional format, after the lesson, the teacher poses a question such as, "What are three words to describe the main character?" Students quickly write three words and then discuss them with their classmates to see if they repeated any words. Distributing the notes, writing, and grouping students take precious class time.

Teachers can use technology to streamline the same activity by quickly creating a simple Google Form. They can reuse the form repeatedly for different questions throughout the year by making a copy for each new question. The teacher shares the link to the form with students through the backchannel or LMS. Students list the three words and press the Submit button. The form compiles the results in a companion spreadsheet.

To make the data more visually interesting, the teacher can highlight and copy the words. Using the website Wordle (www.wordle.net), the teacher can then select *create* and paste in the words. Wordle generates a tag cloud with the words, which become larger the more often they are used. I generated the image in figure 3.1 after asking other teachers and administrators, "What do we want to see students doing or being in our schools?"

Figure 3.1: Wordle image.

Teachers can create Google Forms to collect data from parents, students, and colleagues. They can start by creating a new form, saving it, and selecting a background image. Each question on the form can be a different type—multiple choice, text, scale, grid, and so on. Once the teacher completes it, he or she can share the live form with students.

After students complete the form, the results populate on the teacher's companion spreadsheet. The teacher can sort, search, and manipulate these data. Then they can use a third-party script called Flubaroo (www.flubaroo.com) to grade assignments as soon as students submit them and email back the results. The Flubaroo setup takes some practice, but once the process is in place, it is a huge time saver for teachers.

A Google Form is a good choice for an exit slip for teachers who don't want the whole class to see the answers submitted. On the other hand, using a Google Doc means the students can see everything.

Quiz Using Kahoot!

Kahoot! (https://getkahoot.com) could be the most exciting way yet to collect information from students individually or in groups using technology. Kahoot! is a free website service that works like classroom clickers. The difference between the two is that students don't need a specific clicker; they can use any device that connects to the Internet, including smartphones and tablets.

Teachers start by creating their exit slip questions on the Kahoot! website. Using their devices, students navigate to Kahoot! (https://kahoot.it) and enter the code for the quiz the website generates. Students enter their names, and then the teacher launches the quiz. Students quickly select from the four options, and when everyone has finished, the site reveals a bar graph of the answers. No student names are shown on-screen, but each student receives immediate formative evaluation feedback. The next screen shows the leaderboard of the top five students. This is a perfect exit slip activity because it is fun and fast and provides immediate feedback to the teacher and students.

Kahoot! has a flashy game-show appearance, complete with music throughout the game. Teachers also may insert images or videos into the questions, making it a true multimedia experience. Students enjoy the game-show feel and the competition, and everyone wins because of the immediate feedback. The teacher can download a comprehensive spreadsheet, which details how each student answered the questions, and use it to modify instruction.

Teachers should not have all the fun creating Kahoot! games. Students can create their own games and present them to the class as a review of the content. Some creative ways students have used Kahoot! include:

- Family reunions
- Getting-to-know-me activities
- Interactive curriculum night presentations
- Team-building activities
- Reviews of facts after a presentation

Exit slip activities like these are a valuable educational tool for teachers, and because they are fun, they engage students and allow them to end lessons on a positive note.

The technology tool Kahoot! is a great way to end this chapter and summarize key ideas. You can start Kahooting! tomorrow, but it will only be effective if you engage students by asking higher-level questions and focusing discussions on student results. Rich discussion and immediate feedback are critical thinking processes that can't be rushed. Technology tools will continually change and improve, but it really doesn't matter what technology tools you use. If teachers continue to engage in lower-level discussions and thinking skills, all the music and leaderboards will not help increase student achievement.

⚡ Team Discussion Questions

Use the following questions for personal review, professional development, or as a discussion guide for collaborative groups in your PLC.

1. Of the three strategies introduced to organize reflections, which one do you plan on exploring first, and why?

2. Explain why a naming system is important when using Google Drive, and share an example of what you plan on using.

3. Of the three ways to share audio projects online presented in this chapter, which one will you explore first, and why?

4. What is your opinion on shared note taking in the classroom? Write a paragraph explaining your position.

5. What are your thoughts about the SAMR blog example? How could you apply the ideas to your work?

6. The three-word summary is a great recapping strategy; write a few sentences describing it to a colleague.

7. How could the use of Flubaroo and Google Drive save you time?

8. When gathering feedback from students, when would you choose a Google Form over a Google Doc?

9. The Livescribe Smartpen is amazing technology for creating a pencast. How could you use it in your professional work?

10. Of the options for creating exit slips discussed in this chapter, which solution will you explore first, and why?

CHAPTER 4

Teaching Metacognition With Technology

I am inspired each time I follow #d60learns on Twitter because it shows students' metacognition through the daily broadcasts of short posts and pictures. The hashtag feeds show students' daily work as they scaffold their skills. I worked with the suburban K–8 school district behind this feed to help it make stronger connections among pedagogy, assessment, and digital tools. The teachers and administrators understand good teaching and learning, and they celebrate student work on a daily basis by broadcasting pictures and activities using Twitter as their social media platform.

Across the district, small groups of students collaborate in all subjects, creating projects they often share with students in other classrooms through social media. One of the projects I watched via #d60learns was a screencast by students in the second grade. (As previously described, a *screencast* is a movie created as a student or teacher teaches a lesson using specific apps, software, or websites. The completed movie captures the student or teacher writing and drawing as well as the narration.) The students drew pictures using the screencasting app Explain Everything (http://explaineverything .com). After sequencing the pictures, they narrated the stories, capturing the voice and the action on-screen using the screencasting software. They shared the stories they created with other classes.

After practicing screencasting in professional development, Jack, a middle school mathematics teacher in the district, started creating his own screencasts designed to help students who struggle with specific concepts. Jack floundered with his first few lessons but soon relaxed and let his personality shine through. After completing each lesson, Jack posts his screencasts to his Google Drive and shares them with his classes through his Google Classroom. To create his screencasts, Jack uses the screen recorder feature included in his SMART Board software, making it very natural to teach mathematics content while he records.

After watching their mathematics teacher's screencasts, Jack's students wanted to create their own screencast movies. They use all the technology they can get their hands on, including Chromebooks, iPads, computers, and their phones to create screencasts. They quickly learned that recording screencasts at school is difficult because of the background noise, so many students record at home for better quality.

Jack gives his students the choice to write homework problems on paper or to create a screencast of the selected problems. Most students prefer creating screencasts over copying problems out of the book, so they continue to create and share their screencasts with their classmates and teacher through the Google Classroom platform. Once students gain experience with screencasting, they start to get creative and modify their voices, making the screencasts more of a production. Very quickly, Jack realized that this use of technology gave him more insight into the thinking behind the answers students turned in. Jack started using the screencasts to reteach key concepts, so students could see where they had missed steps in the problem-solving process.

Jack restructured his class to build in time for peer reflection of specific problems, and the students started coaching each other and helping to clarify concepts. They began to think about their own thinking and how they solve problems; the technology tools and apps just help them with the metacognitive process. The idea spread to other classrooms as students taught their other teachers how to create and use screencasts. (J. Williams, personal communication, October 29, 2014)

This chapter presents strategies to help students think about their own thinking—in other words, the metacognitive process. The metacognitive process becomes more complicated with the addition of technology because there are so many solutions and approaches, and the field is always changing. Students of all ages (including teachers) must think about their own thinking and create a plan for how they will approach each learning task.

Exploring Metacognition

In the race to infuse classrooms with technology, most teachers and technology specialists overlook *metacognition*, or thinking about one's own thinking. The focus lands instead on the tools, meaning the available apps, websites, and software. Often in the classroom, teachers decide on the tool for a project with a one-size-fits-all mindset. Students, however, benefit from exposure to a variety of tools and practices using different technologies, as well as reflection on their decisions and thought processes. When a student receives a task or a problem, he or she should undertake the metacognitive process to think about which tool best fits that task.

Despite its benefits, a focus on metacognition has not historically been the practice in most classrooms. In elementary and middle schools of the past, teachers scheduled their students in the computer lab for a short time period each week, where they explored and created something that was usually disconnected from classroom instruction. Projects did not often require higher-level thinking, and students rarely had a choice about how to pursue their projects. Most school districts have replaced the computer lab model with classroom technology. However, many classroom teachers still struggle with integrating the technology part of teaching and learning instead of isolating it.

Letting students explore new tools and create projects using various apps is a new way of thinking for many teachers. Students need practice thinking about their own thinking, and they need to develop the initiative to discover the tools that work best for their purposes. Technology is not the only way to solve a complex problem, and students should be comfortable using a variety of strategies, including paper and pencil, models, and video tutorials on YouTube.

Modeling Metacognition in Professional Development

In my professional practice, I find that educators struggle with their own metacognition as it relates to technology use. Thinking about thinking is a challenge for teachers who struggle just to catch up or keep up with technology hardware, software, and web 2.0 apps. Many teachers still want step-by-step instructions focused on websites, apps, and software. Cheat sheets, as I call them, do not work. That is the old model of professional development for technology.

In the old model, teachers would attend a professional development session, follow the cheat sheet to learn the new technology tool, and then leave without applying what they learned to their work with students. After the session, the teachers would place their notes in the technology binder on the shelf—and change nothing in their instructional practice or curriculum connections.

Teachers now need guided exploration of the tools to connect them with projects students could create with those tools. Professional development is no longer an event; now it's ongoing and personal for each

continued →

educator. Professional development experiences must include thinking about one's own thinking, and this requires time to collaborate and process how teachers can use technology tools in the classroom.

Modeling is as important in professional development as it is in the classroom. Students and teachers need options, meaning a variety of tools, so they can apply their metacognitive strategies to select the appropriate tool as it relates to curriculum, standards, assessment, and student products.

Preparing students for college and careers is a central tenet of education, and teaching metacognition is critical to future success. Students who know how to think about their own thinking can select the appropriate tools to successfully complete real-world tasks. Being able to think about thinking is not just a skill that's nice to have; it is a critical skill for succeeding in this fast-paced world of technology.

Students need time to weigh the options of different technology solutions. They also must be able to use prior knowledge to create a plan for solving problems. Teachers should structure time for students to explore the best technology applications, reflect on and evaluate their work, and, most important, modify the approach as needed.

Modeling and practicing thinking skills is critically important for students in a one-to-one environment. The students, not just the teacher, need to know when to close their laptops and pick up a pencil and paper. For example, while taking notes, a student might choose to use his or her device to take a picture of something for future reflection. The metacognition part is evident when the student fluently uses these tools, moving seamlessly between tasks, applications, and formats. Students should be the drivers in how they organize and explain what they have learned with or without technology.

Teachers should let students be the stars, modeling what they have learned as they explore new tools and technologies. Build a classroom culture of student leadership and reflection by encouraging students to bring in appropriate new tools and applications. Encourage students to document their discoveries by creating screencasts about new applications and saving them to the classroom YouTube channel where others can learn from them.

Creating Screencasts

For many students, explaining their thinking is a challenge because they want to jump right in and start using the technology. Screencasting is one way technology can help students reflect on their thinking processes and modify their approach if needed. Both teachers and students can create screencasts by capturing what takes place on the computer or tablet screen along with the audio explanation of the process. Screencasts combine the audio and the visuals for playback as a movie using any Internet-enabled device, without the need for specialized software.

Through the screencasting process, students capture their thinking using a variety of apps, extensions, websites, and software programs. The teacher plays the screencast to see and hear the problem-solving process the students went through to arrive at a conclusion. Then students can publish screencasts online, opening comments to peers in their own class and an authentic audience outside of the classroom.

Any teacher who has an interactive whiteboard in his or her classroom has the software to create a screencast. Each of the major whiteboard manufacturers includes screen recorder features.

To create your first screencast, press the Record button and teach your lesson. Keep the screencasts short—between three and seven minutes is ideal; longer screencasts create large files that are hard to manage.

Think of the screens as presentation slides that make up the final screencast. These screens can be sequenced in advance before the recording. For example, a teacher could snap a picture of a section of student writing and use that image as the background. Then he or she uses the screencasting tool to write over the student work and narrate feedback to the class. After the lesson is recorded, each application, software resource, and app prompts the user to name and save the screencast.

Examples of Screencasts

- **Khan Academy:** www.khanacademy.org

- **Bozeman Science:** http://goo.gl/Ekv98j

- **Educreations:** www.educreations.com

The Khan Academy, for example, is an online collection of screencasts covering various curriculum topics. YouTube hosts the videos, but the academy organizes them by topic on its website. Khan Academy continues to grow, adding five or more screencasts each day. Google and the Bill and Melinda Gates Foundation have funded the project, which has added practice problems and even the ability for teachers or parents to coach

continued →

students. This resource is available to everyone for free.

The Khan Academy offers a curriculum map that starts with basic mathematics and offers a suggested path to work up to very complicated mathematics. Students can invite a teacher to be a coach; this provides the coach with extensive data about how long the students watch videos and which problems they work on. The site continually generates practice problems until a student successfully completes ten in a row. At that point, he or she is considered proficient in the topic. Students receive energy points and badges as they continue to work, which engages them in the learning process.

Software, Apps, and Websites to Create Screencasts

One software option for screencasts, Jing (www.techsmith.com/jing.html), is a free solution that users can download and install on their computers. Jing enforces a five-minute limit on each screencast. I use Camtasia (http://goo.gl/cr5oJ0) software to create screencasts because it includes editing features that are missing from some of the free apps. However, it is not free; after the thirty-day trial, expect to pay to continue using the service.

There are a number of different apps that teachers can use to create screencasts on an iPad or Android platform. Free options include ShowMe (www.showme .com), and ScreenChomp—iPad only (www.techsmith.com/screenchomp.html). I have used both of them. They have the recording feature and offer various ways to publish user creations. Alternatively, a number of different options are available for a small fee for both iPad and Android platforms. Four apps I use regularly include Explain Everything (http://explaineverything.com), Coach's Eye (www.coachseye.com), DoodleCast (iPad only; doodlecastpro.com), and Educreations (www.educreations.com).

Online, navigate to Screencast-O-Matic (http://screencast-o-matic.com) to imme-diately start creating a screencast. Select the desired screen size to capture and start recording. This option has a fifteen-minute limit. The pro version is an inexpensive option. Screenr (www.screenr.com) is another website for creating a screencast. There is nothing to download, and the site saves the screencasts online. Yet another option to create screencasts is an extension to Google Chrome called Screencastify (www .screencastify.com), which includes a free and a premium version. Screencastify is found in the Google Chrome Web Store and is a good option for students and teach-ers using Chromebooks.

Student-Created Screencasts

Students can use any of these tools to record screencasts individually or with a partner. Student-generated screencasts capture the process students go through to solve a problem, which helps the teacher see what he or she needs to clarify or reteach.

Reflecting on screencasts is another strategy for metacognition. Students can also do this in small groups by comparing the screencasts they created and seeing the different ways a problem can be solved. They also can use screencasts to reflect over a period of time if, for example, they create one screencast per month to demonstrate what they learned during a unit.

Students can submit their work to the teacher by uploading completed screencasts to the classroom LMS, the classroom YouTube channel, or the class blog. Or, if the screencast is published online, students can share the link with the teacher.

Screencasts become digital artifacts that students and teachers can post online and open to comments or share privately for reflection about the thinking process.

Options for publishing student and teacher screencasts include:

- YouTube
- Class blog
- Class website
- Class LMS
- Google Classroom
- Sophia (www.sophia.org) and Educreations (www.educreations.com)

Publishing gets screencasts out to an authentic audience to comment on, which offers teachers another opportunity to model what good comments look like. Teachers should explain how appropriate commenting practices can help the author of the screencast think about his or her own thinking. Students can practice giving each other feedback in the online environment.

It is also important to prepare students for negative comments. In the classroom, the teacher can monitor comments, but outside the classroom, students will likely encounter negative comments and need to be prepared. Teachers can use any negative comments as an opportunity to discuss cyberbullying and appropriate online communication practices. Starting in the primary grades, teachers should remind students that they are creating a digital footprint and must build it up with appropriate digital artifacts and comments.

Publishing screencasts online is the first step; getting students and others to look at the screencasts is the next challenge. One way to encourage others to visit is to track comments on the video screencasts and respond to them. Other incentives for students to visit could include classroom bonus points or other rewards. Making the screencasts part of a homework assignment could be another way to drive traffic to a screencast academy, but teachers who do this should be sure all students have access to the Internet at home as well as a device on which to view the videos.

Screencast Academies

My vision for the future is that every teacher will have his or her own online screencasting academy. Anyone in the world can use free tools to make screencasts and publish them online just as Sal Khan did.

Sal Khan originally created Khan Academy using the YouTube platform, posting screencasts without much of an organizational structure. Today, with the help of many millions of dollars in donations, his team continues to grow the Khan Academy. In contrast, Paul Andersen is a high school science teacher from Bozeman, Montana, who spent a number of years building his own online science academy. Using YouTube, Andersen reaches a huge audience. At the writing of this book, his channel has more than 335,000 subscribers and more than forty million views (Andersen, 2015).

To my knowledge, Andersen does not have a team like the Khan Academy, but he does have a passion for science, and he shares it. He has found a way to get his work out the door so that it can impact millions of learners. The comments on both the Khan Academy and on Andersen's YouTube channel (www.youtube.com/user/boze manbiology) demonstrate that the people who access the videos do not just consume the video content; they also contribute to it.

Looking through the comments on any of these videos, I see evidence of metacognition as users ask questions to clarify their own thinking about the topics. This is the type of learning that happens outside of school. When you create your own academy, this type of higher-order questioning could be going on around your screencasts. You may not immediately hit twenty-five million views, but think of your screencasts as a gift to your students whose learning you are trying to support outside the classroom.

> The term *flipping the classroom* describes when students consume a teacher-created screencast outside of class for homework instead of sitting passively in the classroom listening to a lesson. In a true flipped classroom, when the students come to class, they engage in hands-on learning, labs, and discussions. During class time, the teacher serves as a facilitator, checking comprehension and supporting students as needed. Done correctly, a flipped classroom is a very effective way to cover all types of content. Most flipped classrooms are found in middle and high schools. To learn more about flipping a classroom, visit the Flipped Learning Network (http://flippedclassroom.org).

Creating and Using Graphic Organizers

The use of images and multimedia of all types helps students better understand the content and encourages metacognitive reflection. *Graphic organizers* are just one way to manage more images and help students think about their own thinking. Graphic organizers help students to organize their thinking, compare and contrast ideas, and create the connections between ideas to increase metacognition.

Instead of creating graphic organizers from scratch, first investigate what is available online. Many textbooks are now online, offering graphic organizers connected to their content. Some publishers create graphic organizers that students can manipulate and complete online, while others only offer graphic organizers in PDF form. If only the PDF is available, print one, take a picture of the page to create a graphic, and import the image into one of the screencasting methods covered earlier in the chapter. This makes it possible for students to record their thinking.

The website ReadWriteThink offers many graphic organizers for use in the language arts. Look specifically in the section Student Interactives (www.readwritethink.org /classroom-resources/student-interactives). Another online collection to explore is the website Teachers Pay Teachers (www.teacherspayteachers.com). This site offers free and low-cost resources across all curricular areas for preK–12.

The social network of choice for graphic organizers is Pinterest (www.pinterest .com). Teachers can search by subject area or grade level to discover free resources other teachers have pinned, or posted, to the website. Other people can then pin the resources to their own boards. In my research, I found lots of graphic organizers, many of them linking back to the website Teachers Pay Teachers.

Your computer hard drive might be filled with graphic organizers that you would like to share with students. Traditionally, these organizers would be printed and distributed to students. Using Google Drive, they can be uploaded and shared. Google Drive includes an option to keep files in their native format or to convert them to a Google Doc, spreadsheet, or presentation. Once the files have been uploaded to Google Drive, each document is assigned a unique web address that then can be shared with students.

Within Google Drive, teachers can arrange graphic organizers into folders and share them across grade levels. Each teacher should make a master copy of the graphic organizer before sharing the document with students to keep the original intact.

Some quick ways to create graphic organizers include Microsoft PowerPoint, Microsoft Word, Google Drawings, or one of the many infographic websites. In Microsoft Word, the toolbar with the most features is the Insert toolbar. Options include shapes, flowcharts, and callouts. The same options are available in the

PowerPoint Insert menu, but additionally, PowerPoint includes a host of options in the SmartArt tab. Once the user has created a graphic in PowerPoint, he or she can save the slide in JPG format in the Save As menu, turning the entire slide into a graphic.

Infographics are one type of graphic organizer. Some websites to create infographics include the following.

Piktochart: http://piktochart.com

Infogr.am: https://infogr.am

Easel.ly: www.easel.ly

Visually: http://visual.ly

Pinterest (www.pinterest.com) has the biggest collection of infographics. Search for subject-specific infographics to inspire students to create their own. Creating infographics requires critical thinking and metacognition; students match the data with visuals to create meaningful messages.

Google Drawings is part of Google Drive, and the tools are similar to those available in Word and PowerPoint. The advantage of Google Drive is the ability to share the document. In the classroom, one student could create the graphic organizer and share it with another student to complete the drawing. Involving students in the creation of graphic organizers helps them think about their own thinking.

A number of websites also allow users to create graphic organizers. Most of these offer some features for free, with premium options available for a fee. Creating a graphic organizer is not easy, but using them is a great way for students to think about their own thinking, breaking difficult information into a simplified and visual form.

Comparing and Contrasting Using Whiteboards

There are many different interactive whiteboard brands, including SMART Board, Promethean, Mimio, and StarBoard. The software varies, but each grants the teacher the ability to create templates for students to use to compare and contrast different topics. The software also features built-in galleries of different images. By comparing and contrasting, students can focus on their own thinking, and the graphic organizers help them to organize their thinking into different categories. This process can be done individually, in small groups, or with the whole class. Students heighten their metacognitive thinking by making connections between ideas and synthesizing the ideas of other group members.

I saw this strategy in action in a sixth-grade classroom, as a group of students huddled around an interactive whiteboard creating a graphic organizer about a story they just read. While these students worked, the teacher was across the room working with another group of students. Because the teacher had modeled this metacognitive strategy many times, the students were comfortable comparing and contrasting facts and details as well as their use of whiteboard technology. The group members saved their work and went back to their seats, and then the next group gathered at the whiteboard. I noticed the way students shared the work of recording ideas on the whiteboard by handing the pen to different group members after recording ideas. This routine had obviously been modeled and practiced, because there was no discussion or argument about taking turns at the whiteboard.

Each of the interactive whiteboard brands also offers other teachers' online lesson plans and samples that are available to download and use in the classroom. A search in the SMART Exchange (http://exchange.smarttech.com) shows more than six hundred compare-and-contrast lessons.

Creating Tag Clouds to Compare Themes

A tag cloud is a visual display of information in which the words used most frequently become larger. Chapter 3 described the example of a tag cloud created from a three-word summary exercise. Creating a tag cloud is also a strategy to get students thinking about their own thinking. It's a good way to identify themes, look for big ideas, and visualize information. For ideas on using tag clouds in the classroom, check out the blog post "101 Ways to Use Tagxedo" on the blog *All Things Tagxedo* (Leung, 2010).

Some websites for creating tag clouds include the following.

- **Wordle:** www.wordle.net
- **Tagxedo:** www.tagxedo.com
- **TagCrowd:** http://tagcrowd.com
- **Tagul:** https://tagul.com
- **WordItOut:** http://worditout.com

From screencasting to tag clouds, this chapter covered a wide range of technology tools that can help students and teachers with metacognition—thinking about their own thinking. Not all technology tools apply to all thinking processes. This chapter emphasized that the best way to use technology for metacognition is to find the right technology tool for the task. Students who know how to think about their own thinking should be encouraged to select the appropriate tools to successfully complete any task inside and outside the classroom, whether they be technology tools or something else entirely.

⚡ Team Discussion Questions

Use the following questions for personal review, professional development, or as a discussion guide for collaborative groups in your PLC.

1. How would you best describe the concept of metacognition to someone who has never heard of this concept?

2. What changes need to occur in professional development to help teachers think about their own thinking as it relates to technology?

3. How would you explain screencasting to someone who has never heard the word?

4. Screencasting is a powerful technology for teachers and students. How do you feel you could embed this strategy in your work?

5. This chapter shares three examples of screencast collections. Compare and contrast these collections.

6. What will be your first step in creating a teacher screencast, and what app or website do you plan to explore first?

7. When students create screencasts, they model their thinking. Whom do you think this strategy will help the most given the group you currently work with?

8. From the many options detailed in the section about sharing screencasts, which one do you plan to investigate first, and why?

9. Think about the possibility of creating your own screencasting academy. What will be your starting point, and what are your goals?

10. In what ways can you use graphic organizers and infographics within your curriculum to help students think about their own thinking?

CHAPTER 5

Recognizing and Reinforcing the Efforts of Students, Schools, and Districts

Recognizing achievement is a powerful motivating force. One third-grade teacher shared with me how his students obsess over the badges they earn on the Khan Academy website. He keeps track of the students' activities in his role as a coach. The data analytics are so detailed that a teacher can drill down to specific problems the students missed. In his classroom, students can elect to complete Khan Academy activities in their free time, but he discovered that they did most of the work outside of school.

He noted that one girl was way out in front, well ahead of the pack. From the data, he could see that this student did not watch very many of the videos, but she still successfully completed many of the topics covered in middle school mathematics. He followed up with her to check for understanding and discovered that she loved mathematics and really did understand the advanced topics. The student said she loved earning the badges and was very proud of her accomplishments. The teacher, in turn, met with the curriculum coordinator to create a modified curriculum to meet the needs of this student instead of letting her sit through the third-grade mathematics topics she had already mastered.

In the previous chapter, we talked about students and teachers reflecting on their own thinking. In this chapter, the focus turns to recognition and reinforcement of student efforts, using a blended approach of technology and face-to-face interaction. Educators have countless ways to recognize and reinforce student efforts. Adding powerful technology tools creates even more. Teachers can continue to use traditional feedback strategies while incorporating new digital resources to expand their options and engage more students.

This chapter introduces gamification as a feedback strategy for students, explains new apps and websites, and delves into how teachers of varying grade levels use these resources. It discusses how digital tools can save precious teacher time by organizing and archiving the feedback about each individual student. The chapter also explores digital badges, their role in increasing student achievement, and how they are created, as well as resources for teachers who want to incorporate badges into their classroom recognition and reinforcement systems. It also revisits collaborative note-taking strategies as an important part of reinforcing appropriate behaviors when using online tools. Tracking student behavior is a classroom management task all teachers face, but new technology apps can streamline the process of collecting information, visually organizing the feedback, and generating sharable reports.

Parents, guardians, and friends should share in student recognition. New apps make it easier to share the great things going on in classrooms with students' families and also with the entire connected community. This chapter includes specific websites and apps for recognizing student achievement, even to those beyond the classroom walls.

Exploring the Importance of Recognition

Recognizing the efforts of learners in any situation motivates them and helps to create a positive classroom culture. The more specific the recognition, the more it helps students learn and apply the skills to new situations. As we'll learn in the Khan Academy digital badge story, many students thrive on being recognized for their efforts, and they will continue to push themselves to achieve more. With access to social media and various collaborative technology tools, recognition also can come from experts outside of the classroom.

This is an exciting time to write about the role of technology tools in recognition and reinforcement because new tools and apps are popping up all over the Internet. Luckily, my PLN on Twitter helps me keep up with online developments in this area. I will update the companion website for this book at **go.solution-tree.com/technology** with new resources to keep you on the cutting edge of development.

Teachers can use technology tools, apps, and websites to recognize students and reinforce their efforts in new, visual ways. Many technology solutions streamline the whole cycle of recognition by creating a running record of the feedback that students receive. Some of the current feedback systems also include parents in the feedback loop with automatically generated weekly email reports.

Engaging Learners Through Gamification

Watch a toddler playing an iPad game, and you can see the engagement. The sounds, colors, and movement have that child completely consumed with learning. He or she plays the game to gather points, icons, virtual stickers, and much more. These pint-sized learners engage in learning by playing games; this is called *gamification*.

This doesn't stop with the preschool set. Left on their own, many teenagers would rarely stop playing video games to eat or sleep. These teens not only engage with the video game, they also interact with players around the globe. They must often solve very complex problems to move through the game to the next level. They must collaborate with other players while they do goal-focused work. Gamification is learning while playing.

Adults are not immune to the lure of gamification. How about the teacher who is so obsessed with his or her virtual farm in the app FarmVille that he or she uses a credit card to feed virtual farm animals? Or, what about the neighbor who is so addicted to the game Candy Crush Saga that he or she proudly announces what level he or she is on at each coffee date? Or what about senior citizens using the app Words With Friends to connect with other players, taking the competition to all new levels?

Compare these informal learning examples to a traditional classroom, and the contrast is stunning. No wonder so many students drop out of school. Learning at home has become much more engaging. That is why this section on gamification is critical. Not everything should or will turn into a game, but gamification is a powerful tool, and it is important to understand how it relates to technology, apps, and websites.

Zac Fitz-Walter (2013) shares a brief history of gamification on his blog *Gamification Geek*, starting with the definition. He writes, "Gamification describes . . . framing an activity like a game to make it more motivating. The concept of gamification isn't new, but . . . describing it is." Companies large and small are looking at ways they can use gamification to increase engagement, and the education community is catching on to the trend.

The Khan Academy is a leader in gamification and learning. Other apps, games, and websites offer gamification elements, but the progress details vary from app to app. MIT and other institutions are working to create more learning simulations with advanced gamification elements similar to video games.

The process of recognition and reinforcement is second nature to students, as these naturally occur as students engage in video gaming outside the classroom. Many creative teachers are now breaking their content into quests for students, creating a game-like environment. As students master each quest, they are recognized with a badge of completion. Edutopia (www.edutopia.org), a respected source for articles about education and technology, has developed a series of articles and blog posts about teachers who are pioneers in the gamification movement (www.edutopia.org /blogs/beat/game-based-learning). This resource collection will continue to grow as more educators embrace this type of learning and recognition.

Recognition and reinforcement are central to the gamification movement in K–12 classrooms, and as the pioneers of the movement, students are connecting with other students and experts online. Students and teachers developing gaming experiences are using social media platforms, such as Twitter and Facebook, making it possible to coach students about positive online behaviors while they are working with other groups outside the classroom.

Reinforcing Positive Behavior Online and in the Classroom

Teachers can capture positive student behavior and reinforce expectations with data analytics using free technology tools. One of the best apps to record whole-class behavior and individual student actions is ClassDojo. ClassDojo (www.classdojo.com) is a popular website in K–12 classrooms. In the app, the teacher creates a class and students design fun, colorful avatars by selecting from a vast collection of options. The teacher logs into the website to monitor students and provide real-time feedback to improve engagement and behavior.

For example, students might be working on a task, and the teacher circulates around the room awarding points to individual students or the entire class for good behavior. The app tracks the feedback, and the teacher can generate weekly reports for individual students or the entire class. During my professional development sessions, teachers report that the specific recognition reinforces positive behavior, and parents relate that they love weekly reports about their children's behavior in the classroom. The teacher can keep the data private on any Internet-enabled device. However, he or she also can broadcast the progress of the entire class without identifying individual students. Many teachers use ClassDojo to reinforce positive classroom behaviors.

Teachers use ClassDojo for individual student feedback, general class feedback, or a combination of both. They can generate optional reports and email them to parents, sharing only the information about each individual parent's child and a snapshot of the class results. K–12 teachers report that they love ClassDojo because it streamlines communication among parents, students, and the teacher, saving time and providing critical feedback with just one click and no additional data entry.

Google Forms also provides a way to collect information on specific student behaviors. The teacher can quickly create a personalized Google Form based on the questions it contains. Each question can have a different format, like a scale, multiple choice, text, or selecting from a list. In addition, Google Forms now allows users to insert images and videos. It also offers a whole collection of themes, along with the ability to create custom themes. Each time the teacher uses the form to record behaviors, Google automatically saves the data to a spreadsheet. The seamless integration between the form and the spreadsheet streamlines the entire data collection and analysis process.

Teachers can share the Google Form for recognizing good behavior with the entire staff. They also can identify trends using the data. The administration then has all the data on a single spreadsheet that they can sort and chart to look for patterns.

If a teacher wants to create awards and certificates, Pinterest has an extensive collection of behavioral charts at www.pinterest.com/chamber/behavioral-charts, which can be used for positive reinforcement. Teachers can use these awards and certificates to supplement the forms generated from websites like Class Dojo. Even more are available elsewhere on the web.

Another digital resource to create visually attractive awards and certificates is the website Canva (www.canva.com). This website has fresh, innovative templates of all kinds with great images and graphics to include in a certificate.

Tackk (https://tackk.com) is another great resource for design. The interface is simple yet rich with features. A Tackk is a shared media board students can use to add their own images and media to a project, or from websites such as Instagram or Vine. Once the Tackk is created, Tackk projects can be shared online, and other students can comment on the work as well as add additional media to the project. The Tackk website makes it easy to share student work.

Creating and Using Digital Badges

Badges are digital objects in the form of icons that are posted to webpages or other online environments. Organizations or individuals can create and award badges. Teachers can award badges for mastery of skills, completing a project, or specific knowledge. Badges are yet another way to provide recognition for accomplishments in an online environment.

Here is how digital badges work: an individual or group sets the criteria for a badge, learners complete the tasks, and the individual or group assesses them. If the learner meets the goals, the individual or group awards him or her the badge. The concept is the same as that of Boy Scout or Girl Scout badges. The idea is simple and exploding in popularity in many online communities. For instance, there are formal badge programs by companies like Google, Mozilla, and the Khan Academy. Higher education institutions, like Harvard and MIT, also use badges. They offer select classes for free, and for a small assessment fee, students can earn badges.

Badges are significant because they represent a different way to recognize learners for their accomplishments. The learners control when and where they learn, and they know the specific goals and assessment expectations. If they work hard, they earn the reward of a badge. They can showcase their collections of badges on a digital portfolio or blog. Often, learners earn badges for work outside of the classroom or workplace.

There are still many questions around the concept of digital badges. The badge as a true measure of learning depends on the standards and quality controls set by the organization offering the badge. The public will more widely accept the concept of badges for informal learning, as these organizations do more work to validate the badges and the assessments.

Badges encourage students to learn inside and outside the classroom and offer recognition to those learners who go above and beyond. For some students, the motivation to earn a badge might help them discover a passion and encourage them to learn for the joy of learning.

Developing a class badges system can be as simple as creating an account on a website. The website ClassBadges (http://classbadges.com) is specifically designed for teachers, and the setup is quick and easy. After creating a teacher account and a class, the teacher can start making badges. Students who have earned a badge receive a code that they can use to claim their badge.

The system I use is Credly (https://credly.com). Credly is a website as well as a plugin on the blog platform WordPress. The teacher creates a Credly account and selects from the badges in the library. He or she can also create custom badges. Recognizing the student is the next step in the process. On the Credly website, the teacher selects Give Credit Now and enters the student's email address or captures a redemption code to give to the student. The student then uses the code to claim his or her badge.

Open Badges (http://openbadges.org) by Mozilla is an open-source project that makes it possible for teachers to create and issue badges. This site allows learners to collect badges from multiple sources and organize them into a single backpack. Learners can stack their badges to tell the story of their skills and accomplishments.

Badges also have moved to many different LMSs, including the popular Edmodo (www.edmodo.com). Within the Edmodo environment, teachers can create and issue badges for students, and the site displays them along with all the additional student work, keeping everything in one system. Teachers have the option within Edmodo to invite parents to see the work and badges of their sons and daughters.

Using Applications to Track Student Behaviors

Educators and parents should help students make good choices when they use digital tools, apps, and websites inside and outside of school. They can do this by using positive reinforcement and corrections. Students should be aware of expectations and consequences for online behavior, and teachers should reinforce them continually. Students make mistakes and post items that may be inappropriate. The appropriate teacher reactions and actions are critical when this happens.

For example, if students use a backchannel application like TodaysMeet, and one student posts something the teacher feels is inappropriate, the teacher should address the specific problem with that student and use the example as a teachable moment. Knowing how to act online is a critical college and career skill. Students need to understand that what goes on the Internet stays on the Internet, and what they post today can impact their future. I believe it is the educator's job to help them understand this reality, reinforcing positive interactions whenever possible. With some focus on this issue, teachers can rightly hope that students will remember that lesson long after they leave the classroom.

Unfortunately, many teachers and principals take a punitive discipline approach when things don't go as planned, locking down digital resources. This extreme measure prevents students from learning under the guidance of trusted adults. Educators have to be part of efforts to keep students safe online and to help them make good choices, regardless of the technology platform.

Tracking student behavior is important to appropriately reinforce lessons and recognize improvement. Teachers can use Google Docs to track student work and behavior. The first few times that students use Google Docs, some might include off-task comments, but this behavior usually fades after they learn about revision history and that they are not anonymous.

Another strategy to track student behavior is to create a Google Doc and share it with other professionals in the building who also are monitoring behaviors. For example, a teacher might have a student who sees a number of specialists in the building; a shared Google Doc becomes the communication channel that all those involved with a student's education can access. There is also a running record of conversations around the student's behaviors and hopefully, progress toward changing problematic ones.

The use of a shared document saves time for everyone by organizing all the specific conversations about the student into a central location that anyone can open immediately at a team meeting for review. The current practice of sharing information through email, voice mail, or written notes scatters the essential information. Shared documents unite everyone working on the goals for the student.

Another way to collect, share, analyze, and record data on student behavior is to build a widely shared Google Form focused on discipline. Once a teacher has created the form and shared it with the staff, he or she can share the data collected from the form with the discipline team in the form of a spreadsheet. The team can use the collected data to look for trends, problem locations in the building, dates and times of incidents, and data about individual students. One column in the form can record staff actions as well as parent contact and reactions. This method streamlines data collection, review, and action.

Data collection using the Google tools is not about technology; instead, it is about streamlining information. This makes it possible to provide immediate feedback to students about their behaviors, both good and bad, and to reinforce classroom norms and expectations. Technology can make a real difference for everyone involved in the teaching and learning process by significantly reducing the time between student action and adult reaction.

Teachers can embed technology solutions between face-to-face opportunities in many creative ways. Some create a Google Doc and share it with a student's parents, whom they partner with to modify behavior inside and outside the classroom. This creates a complete running record of communication, all in one place, and organized by date. Teachers and parents can then work together to help the student.

Sharing Good News Beyond Classroom Walls

Teachers and administrators can use all types of media to trumpet the great things they and their students accomplish in their classrooms, letting parents and the community see teaching and learning in action through the use of text, video, and pictures on social media. Technology is just the medium. No one should get stuck thinking that major changes will happen in schools because of a communication platform like Twitter. It is essential for everyone to understand the reasons behind the sharing. Social media is a great way to connect schools with students' families, their communities, and the world by promoting the great work of students and teachers.

The districts that make the biggest gains start with the *why*, so that everyone in the entire system understands the purpose of sharing through social media. The *how* can be taught in professional development. This purposeful broadcasting of student work is not bragging by individual teachers; rather, it captures outstanding teaching and learning across the district in a way that can't be done without technology.

Twitter is a popular platform for districts to share good news. The first step to sharing on Twitter is to select an appropriate hashtag. To understand what a districtwide hashtag could look like, take a look at some of the following examples on Twitter.

- #Leydenpride
- #Cantigue

- #sd113a
- #d60learns

Before announcing the districtwide use of the hashtag, administrators should be sure to review the policies that are in place. Specifically, they should examine the rules for sharing student pictures online and make sure parents or guardians have signed permission forms allowing their children to be photographed. Teachers need to know who they should not photograph.

Once the administrative team has checked and modified all policies as needed, it can lead the way by snapping pictures and sharing news from across the district. Specific professional development might be necessary to ensure the administrative team, teachers, and parents are on the same page. The goal should be to involve the entire community in the sharing of great news.

Sometimes, a classroom teacher needs to share specific information with just the students and their parents, and there are technology tools for that specific goal. Old-school technology communication is email. Yes, the classroom teacher could create a group email of parents and send the message that way. But email is a two-way communication that can slow down a busy teacher. A teacher can set up a weekly email blast to parents, but then he or she must spend time fielding follow-up questions and polite responses. Who has time for more email?

A version of texting is a teacher's secret weapon in combating this problem. The website Remind (www.remind.com) creates a one-way blast to students and parents from any device. This service masks the device name and, more important, the teacher's cell phone number. Remind features make it possible to attach messages and files and add voice comments to personalize the message. The teacher also has evidence of the parent communication in the message history. Classroom teachers love the ease of communication, and parents like the helpful reminders.

The way this free service works is simple: the teacher creates an account for the class, receives a unique code, and shares the code with students and their families. The families opt into the service using an app or by going to the Remind website. Families can select to receive messages through email, text, or both, and they can opt out any time. Once students and their families are connected, the teacher can blast one-way messages. The website also has the ability for students and families to post a stamp in response to a teacher's question. This stamp signals that the teacher's message was received. Parents and teachers who use this service are always eager to share how they love the flow of information and the constant communication. This is also a favorite application for coaches and teachers that lead clubs and organizations.

Whatever recognition system teachers choose, it should be as uncomplicated as possible. Each tool for recognition and reinforcement has a purpose and a place in the classroom, but teachers should be selective. Launching ClassDojo, a badge system, and an LMS at the same time will confuse everyone at first. Try one of the options mentioned in this chapter and grow from there. Many teachers report that everything they need for classroom management, communication, and collaboration is in Edmodo, but no system can meet the needs of every classroom or grade level, so explore and have some fun learning.

⚡ Team Discussion Questions

Use the following questions for personal review, professional development, or as a discussion guide for collaborative groups in your PLC.

1. What is your opinion about recognizing and reinforcing the efforts of students?

2. Explain the term *gamification*, and share your personal opinion about gaming in the classroom.

3. How would you best describe ClassDojo to someone who is unfamiliar with the website?

4. What is your opinion about the current and future use of digital badges?

5. Specifically, which of the digital badge systems would you like to explore first, and why?

6. How are LMSs used for student recognition?

7. What would you do if a student were to break the established class norms while using a website, some software, or an app?

8. Compare and contrast three of the listed social media apps or platforms.

9. Explain how revision history works in Google and how you could use this feature in your work.

10. Twitter reappears in this chapter as a way to broadcast good news. What is your understanding of hashtags, and which educational hashtag would you like to learn more about?

CHAPTER 6

Collaborating and Cooperative Learning

Educators often ask me what effective technology use in the classroom looks like, and my answer is always, "Let's go see teaching and learning in action."

In October 2014, I led a field trip of school leaders, school board members, and parents from one district to another district. The visiting team was surprised to see that in almost every classroom, groups of students worked collaboratively on projects and lessons. In most classrooms, they sat on the floor working or at tables in groups.

In the rooms where students used technology, most groups shared a device instead of working independently with computers or iPads. There was a mix of devices in most classrooms, and students did not seem to have a problem moving among the different technology tools. One principal noted that each time she asked a group what it was working on, group members could state the instructional purpose of the lesson, and there was an objective posted on the whiteboard in all classrooms.

One board member was surprised by the high level of student engagement in the tasks. She was impressed by the district hashtag, which was filled with pictures of in-class activities and student products, and said, "That is what I want happening in our schools." Seeing effective technology use in the classroom helped this group create a vision and start to plan for its own district.

This chapter focuses on helping students to succeed while working collaboratively in groups. It explains the concept of cooperative learning and why students' mastery of the skills required for collaboration is critical to their future success. It covers individual accountability within a group setting, group accountability, and structuring learning environments for group success. This chapter also offers collaboration strategies, tips, and tricks to make classroom group work more successful.

Students leaving our K–12 schools should be proficient in collaboration using technology because more and more colleges and universities are integrating these tools into their curricula. Many top universities in the United States are powered by Google Apps for Education, and the numbers are sure to increase.

This chapter also explores strategies for managing cooperative groups, including technology solutions to create groups and monitor their work. It discusses defining group roles as well as using technology to extend learning beyond the classroom and recording group progress. The chapter includes tips for using multimedia in group work and sharing it with an authentic audience via social media and discusses the use of technology to expand collaboration globally through online forums and the creative use of videoconferencing.

Exploring the Importance of Cooperative Learning

Cooperative learning is not simply seating students in groups and hoping they work together. Cooperative learning involves a collection of instructional strategies, specific skills, and assessments designed to help groups function smoothly as they collaborate. Learning how to work in groups is essential for life outside of school. John Hattie (2012b) addresses the benefits of effective collaboration:

> While much of learning and testing in our schools has been aimed at the individual, more often we learn and live with each other. The effect of peers on learning is high . . . and can be much higher indeed if some of the negative influence of peers is mitigated. (p. 78)

Students, now more than ever before, have to be able to learn in all types of groups, from face-to-face groups to virtual groups scattered across the globe, as collaborative skills are essential for success in college and most careers. Many consider these soft skills, but regardless of what they are called, they have become essential in an increasingly globalized world.

Educators should specifically teach, practice, and assess skills of cooperative learning. They should not assume that students know how to work in a group without formal instruction on strategies, feedback, and assessment. Technology tools and resources can help support group work, but it's important for students to master the people skills of working together.

Understanding Individual and Group Accountability

Everyone has been in a group in which one or two people do all the work, yet the entire group receives the same treatment and recognition at the end of the project or event. Dysfunctional group work happens to people of all ages in classrooms, on committees, and in companies across the globe. Effective teachers and leaders know how to structure group work using fundamental cooperative learning strategies.

One of these strategies is to specifically teach and practice individual and group accountability. Carefully structured, the accountability will be balanced and the group work will be more productive. Accountability assessment should be transparent and actionable, and technology can help with that.

Students must understand what individual accountability looks like in a group project. Those within a group select a role or roles to take during a project, and throughout the process, the teacher monitors their individual contributions to the overall project, providing feedback and redirection as needed.

Clear rubrics can help each group member understand individual expectations as they fit in the context of the larger project. For example, suppose groups in a class are creating multimedia projects. To ensure all students in the group participate in the entire process, not just editing the final product, the teacher creates a master rubric in a Google Sheet and shares it with one student in each group. This document becomes the communication vehicle between group members and the teacher during the cooperative learning project. The teacher and group members pose questions and ask for clarification during the process by using the Comments feature in Google Drive. The teacher can give formative evaluation feedback, specifically focusing on individual accountability.

Groups can use Google Docs to bring them together on the same virtual page in the project. A hyperlink between the Google Sheet and the Google Doc allows the teacher to monitor progress in real time. Students cannot be anonymous in a Google Doc, making it the ideal tool to teach individual accountability. The revision history (located under the File menu) tells all, showing exactly who contributed what to the document. Asking each group member to select a different font and color for his or her contribution is a visual way to address individual accountability.

Once students understand individual accountability and the mechanics of working with an online document, the teacher's focus can shift to group accountability. Again, an online rubric hyperlinked from the initial spreadsheet is a good way to keep the groups organized and focused on the task. During group work, students and teachers can again use comments or the chat feature to clarify expectations and provide ongoing feedback. The rubric should be clear about expectations for the group, focusing on the content and the technology.

Part of the cooperative task is to determine which technology tools the group will use to produce the final project. During this project phase, the groups select the application that best fits the expected outcomes. By practicing individual and group accountability, students and teachers ensure that the groups in which they are involved are more productive.

Managing Collaborative Groups

With accountability covered, let's look at how technology can help the teacher with classroom management strategies during cooperative learning.

The first step is to create groups. Some interesting technology tools can help the teacher with this task. ClassDojo (www.classdojo.com), a classroom management app, includes a feature to generate random groups with a single click.

Another way to quickly create groups is the free app GroupMaker (http://splaysoft .weebly.com/groupmaker.html). In GroupMaker, the teacher enters students' names once and then generates groups with a quick tap on a tablet or phone. Within the teacher app, different group categories are available to choose from, including gender, performance, level, or ethnicity.

The Super Teacher Tools group maker is another tool for quickly generating groups (www.superteachertools.com/instantclassroom/group-maker.php). On this website, the teacher enters the students' names and then uses a variety of available tools, including one to create random groups.

There are so many online resources, from LinkedIn to Instagram, that it's easy to become confused. Keeping everything organized during group work takes practice. If you use an LMS in the classroom, this could serve as a home base for storing all your documents.

Google Drive is another option for organizing group files. To organize groups, the user creates a folder and sets the sharing permissions, allowing all group members to edit. Within the shared folder, one Google Doc can be the directory or master page for other documents and websites. To do this, the user creates a Google Doc and places it in the shared folder. He or she can list the other documents and websites connected to the project and hyperlink all the documents from this main document.

The Teacher's Role During Group Work

Once the teacher has formed cooperative groups and the groups start working, he or she becomes a facilitator, moving around the room to provide feedback and monitor work. The teacher can use any Internet-enabled device to drop into the groups by clicking on the hyperlinked Google Docs and then following up as needed.

Another instructional strategy the teacher can use is a backchannel for questions and answers. The backchannel is an alternative to students raising hands with questions. By using a backchannel this way, the teacher can reflect back on the group's work, adjust the pace of the project, and teach minilessons as needed.

During group work time, the teacher can offer informal observations and connect groups to outside experts, as needed, for the projects. The teacher does not have to be the source of all the expertise in the room. He or she should encourage students to seek help from their peers as well.

Group Progress Monitoring

Technology should save time, helping teachers seamlessly organize conversational threads and documents and archive the process all at the same time. The appropriate technology simplifies progress monitoring. Digital exit slip activities, online check-ins using a website like Padlet, chats in an LMS, and quick polls are all effective methods to monitor group progress.

Exit slips provide teachers with a snapshot of progress as students leave class. The teacher can modify the pace of lessons based on the results of the exit slips. Instead of handing out actual slips of paper, students can use their Internet-connected devices to answer questions in a simple Google Form that summarizes groups' progress.

ExitTicket (http://exitticket.org) is a free website filled with resources to help teachers monitor the progress of groups as well as individual students. ExitTicket has both teacher and student modules that provide real-time data similar to online game statistics. Students can view instant assessment scores and track progress over time, all from a graphic-rich dashboard. ExitTicket makes it possible for students to track their own academic performance, set their own learning goals, and direct their own learning using any Internet-enabled device.

The teacher module shows the entire class and allows teachers to drill down to individual students, all from the graphic-rich dashboard. Teachers may view longitudinal data throughout the year and use those data to differentiate instruction and personalize learning. ExitTicket also includes a built-in item bank of assessment questions as well as an editing feature with a mathematics editing engine.

The social networking website Pinterest (www.pinterest.com) has boards filled with exit slip activities for all grade levels. Many of the pins are pencil-and-paper ideas, but teachers could easily modify them using technology. Visit www.pinterest.com /iamhugs/exit-slip-ideas to explore a few pins.

Padlet (http://padlet.com) is another website that helps teachers get a quick snapshot of the progress of student groups. This free online environment is easy to set up, and students can access the website from any Internet-enabled device. The teacher can post questions, and groups can post project updates. They can use the simple interface for many different tasks in the classroom.

In an LMS like Edmodo, group members can post project updates in the discussion section. Using these features simplifies the teacher's workflow, keeping everything in the same interface and preventing the need to bounce between websites. In most student management systems, a teacher can also create a poll to quickly gather progress information from groups.

Group Progress Recording

A student management system is a good way to record the progress of each group during a cooperative learning project. Another effective method is to use a Google Form. The teacher creates the form with one question for the group name or number and the rest of the questions using the scale-type format (for example, on a scale of one to five). Scale questions work best because Google Forms automatically creates a bar graph with question responses. After creating the Google Form, the teacher can view the bar graphs by opening the response spreadsheet. Under the Form menu, he or she selects Summary of Responses. Google updates this feature in real time when groups submit their information via the Google Form. The teacher could use this information to provide a visual pacing guide for groups.

Group Work Preservation With Multimedia

Teachers can record students during group work, using a phone or a tablet, and put the digital images together in a short video using one of the methods discussed in chapter 2. They also can broadcast these digital images on social media. The images can serve as evidence of the various instructional strategies the teacher uses in the classroom. They also make great additions to a professional portfolio.

Most laptops, tablets, and phones can record audio. The group or teacher can use audio clips for reflection after the lesson as well as to address specific concerns about group participation. The groups should upload audio clips to Google Drive and share the hyperlink for review or for group members who missed class.

Creating Global Cooperative Groups

All of the classroom strategies I covered in the previous section make face-to-face cooperative group work processes more efficient, but what happens when group members are spread out across the globe? Technology tools and web resources make it possible to reach experts in exciting new ways. Creating global cooperative groups is one way to prepare students for the real world of work today and in the future. This sounds like a great idea, but how does a teacher get started?

Microsoft has created Skype in the Classroom (https://education.skype.com) as a way to connect educators who wish to learn together. More than one hundred thousand educators share resources and connect through this website. Interested teachers register and complete their profiles by posting whom they would like to connect with, the grade level, and subject areas. Some teachers look for specific connections, while others just look for other classes to connect with in a more general way.

There is a lot to explore on Skype in the Classroom, including a massive lesson plan bank. For example, a teacher can search for lessons about using Skype to reach other classrooms in different regions of the United States. One third-grade teacher posted a world citizen project. This project runs for the entire school year, and if another teacher is interested in connecting with the third-grade students in Colorado, he or she can join the project.

Videoconferences to Connect Group Members

Skype in the Classroom simplifies the connection to other educators. The lesson bank is filled with creative ways to use videoconferencing in the classroom. However, teachers must install the Skype software on a computer, and this can be a problem if he or she does not have the correct permissions to do so.

There are alternatives, including Google Hangouts, which is a good tool to connect global groups with no software to install. Teachers can access Hangouts via Google Plus, which is available through a Google account. Some districts that use Google Apps for Education may need to enable this feature before they can use Hangouts in the classroom. Up to fifteen people from anywhere in the world can participate in real time in a single Hangout. As with Skype, Hangouts features videoconferencing capabilities as well as chat. FaceTime is yet another option for videoconferences if group members have Apple products like an iPad or iPhone.

Social Media to Connect Group Members

Social media is another way for students to find and connect with group members outside of the classroom. If students are thirteen or older, they may create a Facebook group as a basis for collaboration or a Twitter hashtag to organize the tweets of the group as they work together. If students need digital images for the project, Instagram is another social media option.

Students should practice using social media appropriately to help prepare them for college and career work. A good place to start is on the website LinkedIn. LinkedIn (www.linkedin.com) is a great place to look for subject matter experts. Students can use LinkedIn to find specific people and companies. Students in high school should join LinkedIn and create a profile. As they enter college or move into a career, this social media website can help them make connections and search for job opportunities.

Social media and Google Drive are game changers when it comes to collaborative and cooperative learning in the classroom. The ability to collaborate with different kinds of people and groups is critical to students' future success, and students need specific skills to be prepared. These include skills in both face-to-face and virtual group collaboration. Virtual collaboration and group work can present challenges that face-to-face interactions do not. And although technology tools can help support group work, it's essential for students to master the people skills of working together and understanding individual and group accountability, managing group work, and understanding the best ways to implement technology in the process.

⚡ Team Discussion Questions

Use the following questions for personal review, professional development, or as a discussion guide for collaborative groups in your PLC.

1. What experience do you have working with students in cooperative groups? What are some successes and challenges you have experienced?

2. How can features in Google Docs help students understand individual and group accountability?

3. What is the purpose of student roles when working in cooperative groups?

4. Of the technology tools for creating groups discussed in this chapter, which one do you plan on investigating first, and why?

5. What should the teacher do while students work in cooperative groups?

6. What are some of the strategies a teacher could use to monitor group work?

7. Investigate the website ExitTicket (http://exitticket.org). How could you use this in your professional practice?

8. What are some ways you could capture student interactions when students are working in small groups?

9. Why is it important to create global cooperative groups, and how would you make this work in your classroom?

10. How is the use of social media part of the cooperative group process?

EPILOGUE

LOOKING AHEAD

Michael Fullan's (2013) book *Stratosphere: Integrating Technology, Pedagogy, and Change Knowledge* really helped me shift my thinking, professional practice, and research. I have always connected good teaching and learning with technology, but for many years, I let the web 2.0 tools lead and the pedagogy follow. I was able to make a clear connection to the pedagogy in my mind's eye, but I noticed participants in my session were not making the same instructional connections.

Many of the teachers in my coaching and professional development sessions fell short of instructional connections because they were stuck in the features or functions of the technology tool I was sharing. The mighty newcomer to the formative assessment arena, Kahoot!, a game-like website to engage students, is a good example for illustrating this phenomenon. Teachers and students alike get so caught up in the gamification features, like leaderboards, music, and fast pace, that they forget to focus on higher-order questioning and analysis of the collected data. The features and glitz of the tool can consume teachers so much that they lose sight of the *purpose* of the technology. Administrators are excited after a professional development session because they see and hear the cheering as teachers start Kahoot!ing in the classroom.

Professional development in instructional strategies can be a powerful force for positive change, but it has to be for the right purpose in the right context. Pedagogy must lead the use of technology; if it does not, Kahoot! is nothing more than drill and kill wrapped up in fancy digital flashcards! In other words, drilling students with low-level questions to recall information leads to killing their motivation to learn. The questions used in the Kahoot! session must address higher-order thinking skills.

After a few Kahoot!ing experiences like this, I reframed the reason for this instructional strategy, stating as often as possible that it is not about the app, website, or device; it is all about the pedagogy. Throughout this book, I have emphasized that the curriculum must dictate the technology tools, and the need for change shifts around pedagogy, assessment, and everything else.

Teachers must continue to look ahead to possibilities for teaching and learning in a digitally rich world. Certain concepts will remain the same, including the importance of collaboration in a constantly changing world and the value of quality feedback, regardless of the technology platform. Tools, apps, software, and websites are in constant flux; the only constant is change itself, so educators must keep pedagogy at the forefront.

The following appendix lists all the technology resources from the book, along with a short summary of each app, website, software, or platform. As noted previously, I will add and update tools on the companion website (**go.solution-tree.com/technology**) for the book. Let's continue to learn together!

# APPENDIX

TECHNOLOGY RESOURCES

This resource collection is intended as a handy summary, not a comprehensive guide. Many of the tools are multifunctional. I have focused on Internet-based tools rather than hardware—with a few exceptions.

- **Adobe Photoshop Elements (www.adobe.com/products/photoshop -elements.html):** Software for creating and editing images
- **Animoto (https://animoto.com):** Website and app to create videos
- **Audacity (http://audacity.sourceforge.net):** Software to edit audio
- **AudioNote (https://itunes.apple.com/us/app/audionote-notepad-voice -recorder/id369820957?mt=8):** Apple app to record notes
- **Blackboard (www.blackboard.com):** Comprehensive learning management platform with many add-on options
- **Blogger (www.blogger.com):** Google's blogging platform
- **Bozeman Science (http://goo.gl/Ekv98j):** Good example of how a teacher organizes screencasts on his YouTube channel
- **Camtasia (http://goo.gl/cr5oJ0):** Screencasting software
- **Canva (www.canva.com):** Website to create posters, fliers, and more
- **Canvas (www.canvaslms.com):** Learning management system (LMS)
- **ClassBadges (http://classbadges.com):** Badge system specifically created for teachers
- **ClassDojo (www.classdojo.com):** Student behavior management system
- **Coach's Eye (www.coachseye.com):** Video app that replays all action in slow motion
- **CompareNContrast (https://itunes.apple.com/us/app/comparecontrast /id578513815?mt=8):** App to compare and contrast

- **Credly (https://credly.com):** System to create badges
- **Do Ink (www.doink.com):** App to create videos
- **Doodlecast (http://doodlecastpro.com):** Screencasting app available for the iPad only
- **Dropbox (www.dropbox.com):** Online storage and file-sharing solution
- **Easel.ly (www.easel.ly):** Website to create infographics
- **Edmodo (www.edmodo.com):** LMS complete with badges
- **Edublogs (http://edublogs.org):** Blogging platform for educators
- **Educational hashtags (www.cybraryman.com/edhashtags.html):** Comprehensive list of educational hashtags
- **Educreations (www.educreations.com):** App and website to create and store screencasts
- **Evernote (https://evernote.com):** Workspace app usable on any Internet-connected device
- **ExitTicket (http://exitticket.org):** System to create exit tickets and manage responses
- **Explain Everything (www.morriscooke.com/applications-ios/explain-everything-2):** App to create screencasts
- **Facebook (www.facebook.com):** Social media platform to share images, videos, and links (for students thirteen and older)
- **FaceTime (www.apple.com/mac/facetime):** App to make video calls between Apple devices
- **Flickr Advanced Search (www.flickr.com/search/advanced):** Website to search archives of images uploaded by other users
- **Flipped Learning Network (http://flippedclassroom.org):** Community of educators learning about the flipped classroom
- **Flubaroo (www.flubaroo.com):** Script to create self-graded quizzes in Google Forms
- **GarageBand (www.apple.com/mac/garageband):** Apple software for editing music
- **Gmail (https://mail.google.com):** Email platform by Google
- **Google Advanced Search (www.google.com/advanced_image_search):** Website to narrow search topics

- **Google Classroom (https://classroom.google.com):** Document management platform for Google Apps for Education schools

- **Google Docs (www.google.com/docs/about):** App for word processing

- **Google Drawings (www.google.com/edu/training/get-trained/drawings/introduction.html):** App to create drawings

- **Google Drive (https://drive.google.com):** Suite of Google tools that includes word processing, spreadsheets, presentations, forms, and drawings

- **Google Forms (www.google.com/forms/about):** App to create surveys, quizzes, and polls

- **Google Hangouts (www.google.com/+/learnmore/hangouts):** App and software to create a hangout, invite friends to videoconferences, share files, and chat

- **Google Sheets (www.google.com/sheets/about):** App to create spreadsheets

- **Google Slides (www.google.com/slides/about):** App to create presentations

- **GoPro (http://gopro.com):** A series of digital cameras and mounts to create wearable technology for filming

- **GroupMaker (http://splaysoft.weebly.com/groupmaker.html):** Free app to create a group

- **Haiku Deck (www.haikudeck.com):** Software to create stunning presentations

- **ImageChef (www.imagechef.com):** Website to create new images by adding text to an existing image

- **iMovie (www.apple.com/mac/imovie):** Apple software to create videos

- **Incompetech (http://incompetech.com/music/royalty-free):** Collection of free music

- **Infogr.am (https://infogr.am):** Infographic generator

- **iTunes (www.apple.com/itunes):** Site to upload student-created podcasts

- **Jing (www.techsmith.com/jing.html):** Free software to create short screencasts

- **Kahoot! (https://getkahoot.com):** Student response system

- **Kaizena (https://kaizena.com):** Add-on for Google Drive, making it possible to leave voice comments in Google Docs

- **Khan Academy (www.khanacademy.org):** Free website with videos and practice problems, covering everything from mathematics to government

- **Kidblog (http://kidblog.org):** Blogging platform for students

- **Library of Congress (http://memory.loc.gov/ammem/index.html):** Collection of images (check each collection for copyright information); students can use most images in their projects

- **LinkedIn (www.linkedin.com):** Social media platform used mainly in business to create groups and networks

- **Livescribe Smartpen (www.livescribe.com/en-us):** Special pen that captures what users write, draw, and hear

- **MimioConnect (www.mimioconnect.com):** Brand of interactive whiteboards

- **Mobygratis (www.mobygratis.com):** Free music collection

- **My Big Campus (www.mybigcampus.com):** LMS

- **NASA image gallery (http://nix.nasa.gov):** Image collection (most images not copyrighted)

- **NOAA Photo Library (www.photolib.noaa.gov):** Great collection of images about nature and weather

- **OneNote (www.onenote.com):** Software to share notes among all of one's devices

- **Open Badges (http://openbadges.org):** System to create badges

- **Padlet (https://padlet.com):** Platform to collaborate online

- **PBworks (www.pbworks.com):** Platform to create a wiki

- **Picasa (http://picasa.google.com):** Software to edit and share digital images

- **Pics4Learning (www.pics4learning.com):** Copyright-friendly image library for teachers and students

- **Piktochart (http://piktochart.com):** Website to create infographics

- **Pinterest (www.pinterest.com):** Social media platform to share images in the form of pins

- **Pixlr (http://pixlr.com):** App to edit images on Apple and Android devices

- **PixyMe (www.pixyme.com):** iPad app to create personalized images

- **Plickers (www.plickers.com):** Paper-based student response system

- **Podbean (www.podbean.com):** Hosting for podcasts

- **PodOmatic (www.podomatic.com):** Website to create and post podcasts

- **Poll Everywhere (www.polleverywhere.com):** Live polling to connect with an audience

- **Promethean (www.prometheanplanet.com/en-us):** Brand of interactive whiteboards

- **ReadWriteThink (www.readwritethink.org/classroom-resources /student-interactives):** Collection of graphic organizers

- **Remind (www.remind.com):** Way to send messages to families and students

- **RoyaltyFreeMusic.com (www.royaltyfreemusic.com):** Collection of free music clips

- **Schoology (www.schoology.com):** Learning management platform

- **Screencastify (www.screencastify.com):** Google Chrome browser extension to create screencasts

- **Screencast-O-Matic (www.screencast-o-matic.com):** Website to create short screencasts

- **ScreenChomp (www.techsmith.com/screenchomp.html):** iPad-only app to create screencasts

- **Screenr (www.screenr.com):** Website to create screencasts

- **ShowMe (www.showme.com):** Free app to create screencasts

- **Skype (www.skype.com/en):** Software and app for video calls and chats

- **Skype in the Classroom (https://education.skype.com/lessons):** Collection of projects and lesson plans for using Skype in education

- **SMART Exchange (http://exchange.smarttech.com):** Software for use with interactive whiteboards

- **Socrative (www.socrative.com):** Formative assessment tool

- **Sophia (www.sophia.org):** Website to publish screencasts

- **StarBoard (http://psg.hitachi-solutions.com/starboard):** Brand of interactive whiteboards

- **Stockvault (www.stockvault.net):** Website with free stock photos for personal, noncommercial use

- **Storify (https://storify.com):** Website to archive tweets from a user or a group hashtag

- **SuperTeacherTools Group Maker (www.superteachertools.com /instantclassroom/group-maker.php):** Website to create groups

- **Tackk (https://tackk.com):** Website to create projects using a mix of media

- **TagCrowd (http://tagcrowd.com):** Website to create tag clouds

- **Tagul (https://tagul.com):** Website to create tag clouds

- **Tagxedo (www.tagxedo.com):** Website to create tag clouds

- **Teachers Pay Teachers (www.teacherspayteachers.com):** Online marketplace of resources for teachers

- **TinyURL (http://tinyurl.com):** Website to shorten website addresses

- **TodaysMeet (https://todaysmeet.com):** Free website to create a backchannel to use with a group

- **Twitter (https://twitter.com):** Social media microblogging platform to share pictures, links, and messages with followers

- **Ustream (www.ustream.tv):** Website to broadcast videos

- **Vimeo (https://vimeo.com):** Website to post and view user-created videos

- **Visually (http://visual.ly):** Website to create infographics

- **VoiceThread (https://voicethread.com):** Website to create presentations and invite comments

- **WeVideo (www.wevideo.com):** Website to create and edit videos collaboratively

- **Wikispaces (www.wikispaces.com):** Wiki platform

- **WordItOut (http://worditout.com):** App to create tag clouds

- **Wordle (www.wordle.net):** Tag cloud generator

- **YouTube (www.youtube.com):** Social media platform focused on delivering user-created videos

REFERENCES AND RESOURCES

Andersen, P. (2015). *Bozeman Science*. Accessed at www.youtube.com/user/bozemanbiology/about on September 22, 2015.

Azzam, A. M. (2014). Motivated to learn: A conversation with Daniel Pink. *Educational Leadership*, *72*(1), 12–17.

Bebell, D., & Kay, R. (2010). One to one computing: A summary of the quantitative results from the Berkshire Wireless Learning Initiative. *Journal of Technology, Learning, and Assessment*, *9*(2), 1–59.

Bebell, D., & O'Dwyer, L. M. (2010). Educational outcomes and research from 1:1 computing settings. *Journal of Technology, Learning, and Assessment*, *9*(1), 1–15.

Belgrad, S., Burke, K., & Fogarty, R. (2008). *The portfolio connection: Student work linked to standards* (3rd ed.). Thousand Oaks, CA: Corwin Press.

Bellanca, J. A., & Brandt, R. (Eds.). (2010). *21st century skills: Rethinking how students learn*. Bloomington, IN: Solution Tree Press.

Bellanca, J. A., & Fogarty, R. (1991). *Blueprints for thinking in the cooperative classroom* (2nd ed.). Palatine, IL: Skylight.

Bender, W. N. (2012). *Differentiating instruction for students with learning disabilities: New best practices for general and special educators* (3rd ed.). Thousand Oaks, CA: Corwin Press.

Bransford, J. D., Brown, A. L., & Cocking, R. R. (Eds.). (1999). *How people learn: Brain, mind, experience, and school*. Washington, DC: National Academies Press.

Brookhart, S. M. (2008). *How to give effective feedback to your students*. Alexandria, VA: Association for Supervision and Curriculum Development.

Brookhart, S. M. (2012). Preventing feedback fizzle. *Educational Leadership*, *70*(1), 24–29.

Chapman, C., & King, R. (2009). *Differentiated instructional strategies for reading in the content areas* (2nd ed.). Thousand Oaks, CA: Corwin Press.

Chappuis, J. (2012). "How am I doing?" *Educational Leadership*, *70*(1), 36–41.

Cloud computing. (n.d.). In *Merriam-Webster's online dictionary*. Accessed at www.merriam-webster.com/dictionary/cloud%20computing on April 20, 2015.

Cornelius-White, J. H. D., & Harbaugh, A. P. (2010). *Learner-centered instruction: Building relationships for student success*. Thousand Oaks, CA: SAGE.

Costa, A. L. (2008). *The school as a home for the mind: Creating mindful curriculum, instruction, and dialogue* (2nd ed.). Thousand Oaks, CA: Corwin Press.

Creative Commons. (n.d.). *About the licenses.* Accessed at www.creativecommons.org/licenses on October 27, 2015.

DuFour, R., DuFour, R., & Eaker, R. (2008). *Revisiting professional learning communities at work: New insights for improving schools.* Bloomington, IN: Solution Tree Press.

DuFour, R., DuFour, R., Eaker, R., & Karhanek, G. (2010). *Raising the bar and closing the gap: Whatever it takes.* Bloomington, IN: Solution Tree Press.

Ferriter, W. M. (2014, November 11). *Are there WRONG ways to use technology?* [Weblog post]. Accessed at www.solution-tree.com/blog/wrong-ways-to-use-technology on November 11, 2014.

Ferriter, W. M., & Garry, A. (2010). *Teaching the iGeneration: 5 easy ways to introduce essential skills with web 2.0 tools.* Bloomington, IN: Solution Tree Press.

Ferriter, W. M., Ramsden, J. T., & Sheninger, E. C. (2011). *Communicating and connecting with social media.* Bloomington, IN: Solution Tree Press.

Fisher, D., & Frey, N. (2012). Making time for feedback. *Educational Leadership, 70*(1), 42–46.

Fitz-Walter, Z. (2013, January 24). *A brief history of gamification* [Weblog post]. Accessed at zefcan.com/2013/01/a-brief-history-of-gamification on April 20, 2015.

Fullan, M. (2013). *Stratosphere: Integrating technology, pedagogy, and change knowledge.* Toronto, Ontario, Canada: Pearson.

Fullan, M., & Donnelly, K. (2013). *Alive in the swamp: Assessing digital innovations in education.* London: Nesta. Accessed at www.nesta.org.uk/sites/default/files/alive_in_the _swamp.pdf on April 16, 2015.

Fullan, M., & Langworthy, M. (2013). *Towards a new end: New pedagogies for deep learning.* Seattle, WA: Collaborative Impact.

Godin, S. (2008). *Tribes: We need you to lead us.* New York: Portfolio.

Gordon, J. (2007). *The energy bus: 10 rules to fuel your life, work, and team with positive energy.* Hoboken, NJ: Wiley.

Gregory, G. H. (2008). *Differentiated instructional strategies in practice: Training, implementation, and supervision* (2nd ed.). Thousand Oaks, CA: Corwin Press.

Gregory, G. H., & Chapman, C. (2013). *Differentiated instructional strategies: One size doesn't fit all* (3rd ed.). Thousand Oaks, CA: Corwin Press.

Hattie, J. (2009). *Visible learning: A synthesis of over 800 meta-analyses relating to achievement.* New York: Routledge.

Hattie, J. (2012a). Know thy impact. *Educational Leadership, 70*(1), 18–23.

Hattie, J. (2012b). *Visible learning for teachers: Maximizing impact on learning.* New York: Routledge.

Hattie, J., & Timperley, H. (2007). The power of feedback. *Review of Educational Research, 77*(1), 81–112.

Hord, S. M. (Ed.). (2004). *Learning together, leading together: Changing schools through professional learning communities.* New York: Teachers College Press.

Johnston, P. H. (2012). *Opening minds: Using language to change lives.* Portland, ME: Stenhouse.

Leung, H. (2010, August 9). *101 ways to use Tagxedo* [Weblog post]. Accessed at http://blog.tagxedo .com/101-ways-to-use-tagxedo-completed on April 20, 2015.

Livescribe (n.d.). *What is a pencast?* Accessed at www.livescribe.com/en-us/pencasts on July 6, 2015.

Microsoft. (2015). *Microsoft OneNote in the classroom.* Accessed at www.microsoft.com/education /en-sg/teachers/guides/Pages/one-note.aspx on September 2, 2015.

Pearlman, B. (2009). Making 21st century schools: Creating learner-centered schoolplaces/ workplaces for a new culture of students at work. *Educational Technology, 49*(5), 14–19.

Pogrow, S. (2009). *Teaching content outrageously: How to captivate* all *students and accelerate learning, grades 4–12.* San Francisco: Jossey-Bass.

Puentedura, R. (2006). *Transformation, technology, and education.* Accessed at www.hippasus.com /resources/tte on October 7, 2015.

Puentedura, R. (2014). *SAMR, learning, and assessment.* Accessed at www.hippasus.com/rrpweblog /archives/000139.htm on October 7, 2015.

Robinson, K. (2009). *The element: How finding your passion changes everything.* New York: Penguin.

Schiller, S. Z. (2009). Practicing learner-centered teaching: Pedagogical design and assessment of a second life project. *Journal of Information Systems Education, 20*(3), 369–381.

Speck, M., & Knipe, C. (2001). *Why can't we get it right?: Professional development in our schools.* Thousand Oaks, CA: Corwin Press.

Taranto, G., Dalbon, M., & Gaetano, J. (2011). Academic social networking brings web 2.0 technologies to the middle grades. *Middle School Journal, 42*(5), 12–19.

Tate, M. L. (2010). *Worksheets don't grow dendrites: 20 instructional strategies that engage the brain* (2nd ed.). Thousand Oaks, CA: Corwin Press.

Tate, M. L. (2012). *"Sit and get" won't grow dendrites: 20 professional learning strategies that engage the adult brain* (2nd ed.). Thousand Oaks, CA: Corwin Press.

Tomlinson, C. A. (2003). *Fulfilling the promise of the differentiated classroom: Strategies and tools for responsive teaching.* Alexandria, VA: Association for Supervision and Curriculum Development.

Tomlinson, C. A., & McTighe, J. (2006). *Integrating differentiated instruction and understanding by design: Connecting content and kids.* Alexandria, VA: Association for Supervision and Curriculum Development.

Tovani, C. (2012). Feedback is a two-way street. *Educational Leadership, 70*(1), 48–51.

Visible Learning. (2015). *Glossary of Hattie's influences on student achievement.* Accessed at www .visible-learning.org/glossary on October 5, 2015.

Waack, S. (2013, February 21). *Glossary of Hattie's influences on student achievement.* Accessed at http://visible-learning.org/glossary on April 20, 2015.

Waack, S. (2014, September 12). *Hattie ranking: Influences and effect sizes related to student achievement.* Accessed at http://visible-learning.org/hattie-ranking-influences-effect-sizes-learning-achievement on December 3, 2013.

Wald, P. J., & Castleberry, M. S. (Eds.). (2000). *Educators as learners: Creating a professional learning community in your school.* Alexandria, VA: Association for Supervision and Curriculum Development.

Wiggins, G. (2012). Seven keys to effective feedback. *Educational Leadership, 70*(1), 10–16.

Wiliam, D. (2011). *Embedded formative assessment.* Bloomington, IN: Solution Tree Press.

Wiliam, D. (2012). Feedback: Part of a system. *Educational Leadership, 70*(1), 30–34.

Willis, J. (2011, April 14). *A neurologist makes the case for the video game model as a learning tool* [Weblog post]. Accessed at www.edutopia.org/blog/neurologist-makes-case-video-game-model-learning-tool on April 20, 2015.

INDEX

Solutions for Digital Learner–Centered Classrooms series

Gain practical, high-impact strategies to enhance instruction and heighten student achievement in 21st century classrooms. Using tech-based tools and techniques, your staff will discover how to motivate students to develop curiosity, become actively engaged, and have a sense of purpose in their education.

BKF691, BKF680, BKF636, BKF679, BKF681, BKF664, BKF666

Creating a Digital-Rich Classroom
Meg Ormiston

Design and deliver standards-based lessons in which technology plays an integral role. This book provides a research base and practical strategies for using web 2.0 tools to create engaging lessons that transform and enrich content.

BKF385

Teaching the iGeneration
William M. Ferriter and Adam Garry

Find the natural overlap between the work you already believe in and the digital tools that define today's learning. Each chapter introduces an enduring life skill and a digital solution to enhance traditional skill-based instructional practices. A collection of handouts and supporting materials ends each chapter.

BKF671

Deeper Learning
Edited by James A. Bellanca

Education authorities from around the globe draw on research as well as their own experience to explore deeper learning, a process that promotes higher-order thinking, reasoning, and problem solving to better educate students and prepare them for college and careers.

BKF622

Solution Tree | Press
a division of

Solution Tree

Visit solution-tree.com or call 800.733.6786 to order.

Wait! Your professional development journey doesn't have to end with the last pages of this book.

We realize improving student learning doesn't happen overnight. And your school or district shouldn't be left to puzzle out all the details of this process alone.

No matter where you are on the journey, we're committed to helping you get to the next stage.

Take advantage of everything from **custom workshops** to **keynote presentations** and **interactive web and video conferencing**. We can even help you develop an action plan tailored to fit your specific needs.

Let's get the conversation started.

Call 888.763.9045 today.

solution-tree.com